GROUNDWORK

*A Practitioner's Guide to Building
Alternative Education Programs*

F.M. GANN

iUniverse, Inc.
Bloomington

Groundwork
A Practitioner's Guide to Building Alternative Education Programs

iUniverse books may be ordered through booksellers or by contacting:

iUniverse
1663 Liberty Drive
Bloomington, IN 47403
www.iuniverse.com
1-800-Authors (1-800-288-4677)

ISBN: 978-1-4502-9142-2 (pbk)
ISBN: 978-1-4502-9143-9 (cloth)
ISBN: 978-1-4502-9144-6 (ebk)

Library of Congress Control Number: 2011901494

Printed in the United States of America

iUniverse rev. date: 3/22/2011

Contents

Chapter 1 1
Foundation Questions

Chapter 2 12
Criteria for Implementation

Chapter 3 23
Components of a True Alternative Educational Program

Chapter 4 41
Positive-Based Disciplinary Practices

Chapter 5 64
Alternative Education Programs in Support Of Traditional Schools

Chapter 6 72
Program Longevity: The Art of Survival

Chapter 7 79
Soap Box Discussions

Introduction

This book serves as an experiential guide for school districts considering the implementation of an Alternative Education Program. The information contained in this book is based on the experiences of the author who founded four successful Alternative Educational Programs in both urban and rural settings, serving as both administrator and classroom teacher in each. Written from the perspective of both a program administrator and a day-to-day classroom teacher gives the author the freedom to comment from both perspectives in addressing the challenges posed by at-risk students, their parents, fellow teachers, the community, and district office officials.

Preface

In theory Alternative Education Programs exist to provide students who have experienced personal, social, and academic failure a second chance at success. Creating an educational environment which allows a student a voice in determining educational outcomes and is challenged by the staff to change those things that led to previous school-related failure, is the foundation of such a program. Furthermore, creating an environment in which the student is expected to assume personal responsibility for individual behavior while providing the individual student a framework from which the necessary skills can be developed to achieve personal success within the school setting, remains paramount. School-related success, once internalized, strengthens the student's personal investment in the school and serves to reinforce the commitment of attaining the goal of earning a high school diploma.

In reality many Alternative Education Programs are punitive. They exist to provide school districts with the educational option of removing students from their educational environments for the duration of their school careers. Students whose disruptive classroom behaviors, chronic absenteeism, and continued academic failure are viewed by some district administrators as a detriment to the good order and operation of their schools. Once a student is identified and labeled "at-risk", he is routinely assigned to a district's alternative program. With few exceptions, these programs serve as holding facilities for students until they voluntarily separate themselves from the district, are removed for serious violations of the district's disciplinary code, or graduate from a GED or other academic program offered by the district in lieu of a traditional high school diploma.

In an educational career spanning more than three decades, I have watched public education experts struggle to find educational alternatives for those students who, for whatever reason, can't keep up, don't get it, or require a different approach to classroom instruction. A school district's reliance on Professional Learning Communities and Differentiated Learning Initiatives, while well-intentioned, often have little relevance or practical application when dealing with at-risk students in large, public high schools devoid of strong positive student-teacher relationships. The public school's continued adherence to teacher directed modes of instruction and its reliance on assessment scores as the primary means for determining the quality of a student's educational experience, has resulted in charges of assessment irrelevance, widespread student dissatisfaction, and dwindling public support. The increasingly authoritarian posture of public schools, as evidenced by the widespread adoption of zero tolerance policies, coupled with districts paring down of curriculums, (what is not tested, is not taught) has resulted in an ever widening chasm between the expectations of the educational environment and the expectations of society. True Alternative Education Programs should offer opportunities for individual students to achieve meaningful personal, social, and academic success in an environment characterized by acceptance, support, and positive based discipline.

Based on this philosophy, I founded the Blue Valley Academy in 1998 and served as the program's administrator and classroom teacher for eleven years. The program, located in Overland Park, Kansas continues to serve as the Blue Valley School District's Alternative Educational setting for its at-risk population. From 1998 through 2009, the program served a total of 1,119 at-risk students and achieved a 91% graduation rate, graduating 408 students out of a possible 446 eligible to receive their diplomas. Throughout this period, 990 students or 88% of all enrolled students completed the program for the years they were enrolled. The Academy program was designed as a "second chance" school for students, grades 10-12, who were experiencing little if any school-related success and were in danger of leaving the school environment prior to graduation.

Throughout my tenure as the program's principal and classroom teacher, students often shared their personal perceptions of the program through interviews conducted by the district's Communications Department and through reflections written in their classes. The following student comments are representative of my experience with how students attending alternative programs perceive the experience.

What's It Like To Be An Academy Kid?

"I pretty much gave up on Blue Valley High School before coming to the Academy. Going to school was just getting harder and harder every day that passed. I always felt I was behind, and I had no way to get caught up which made me feel like going to school was pointless. At the Academy, I feel I am going to get something done. I know I'm going to learn something. Teaching is done differently at the Academy. All home school teachers gave assignments without really explaining them and basically said, Here do it. It is easier for me at the Academy because there are fewer kids, and I've found that the teachers know how to explain assignments in my language and make sure all the students understand the work before we begin working. Coming to Blue Valley Academy has always felt like home. I am no longer under pressure and I will graduate" (*J. senior, 2005*)

"When some kids first enter the alternative education program they think that it is a joke. I know many people are unwilling to hear from alternative education kids because they think we aren't worth the extra money our program requires. They think we are sent to this school because no one else wants us. But once a student has been in the program a couple of weeks, they start to notice their grades increasing and classes filled with learning. They are never sitting alone at a desk confused and frustrated. Being part of an alternative education has really changed my view on education and life. I wake up in the morning ready to learn. Before I entered the alternative program, I woke up every morning trying to just get through the day" (*S. senior, 2007*)

"Without the Academy, I would not be graduating this year. The Academy helped me catch up on the credits I needed and helped me get good grades. I go to school every day. I have no one telling me to go, I just go on my own. The Academy taught me that if I just sit and do nothing with my life, I will have nothing" (*T. senior, 2009*)

"The Academy is a turning point. At my home school, I was lost and confused. I wasn't reaching my goals, and I gave up on myself and the idea of graduating. At the Academy, the teachers help me and care about me. It is a lot easier to reach my goals in every class at the Academy because the school has a bigger support system, and I feel like I matter" (*L. sophomore, 2008*)

"The Academy gives me incentive and motivation to create hope in my life. The Academy gives me something to look forward to and gives me important life lessons that I haven't been able to learn in any other environment. I have found my own route to happiness through this school. I'm taking care of myself, making wiser decisions with the guidance, help, and motivation I have gained from people who care about me" (*D. senior, 2009*)

"The teachers at Blue Valley Academy support me. Because of that support, I can make better decisions on what I do. And then, as if it is a chain reaction, I can be happy and help others the same way I have learned to help myself. In doing that, life is better for everyone" (*G. sophomore, 2007*)

Who Should Read This Book?

Classroom teachers and school administrators, who work with their district's At-Risk population and are searching for possible alternatives to their current disciplinary philosophies, program structure, and instructional approaches with regard to their existing programs should read this book.

School district administrators, who are in the planning and design stages prior to the implementation of an Alternative Educational Program in their respective districts, should read this book.

Classroom teachers and building principals, who are struggling to find alternatives to ineffective, punitively oriented, policy-driven disciplinary responses as a means of dealing with the chronic student misbehavior of a few "hard noses" for whom their classrooms and offices have become daily battle grounds, should read this book.

CHAPTER 1

Foundation Questions

All true alternative education programs exist for one fundamental purpose; to make a positive difference in a kids life.

Throughout the process of creating four alternative educational programs (AEP), I have found that school district's planning to implement an AEP should focus on four basic questions. Once these questions have been satisfactorily answered by the district's stakeholders, a format for moving forward in the process will be set.

1. Whom will the program serve?

2. How will students be referred to the program?

3. How will the program be evaluated?

4. How will the district inform the public and promote the program?

Whom Will The Program Serve?

(Characteristics of Intended Population)

District stakeholders must first determine the mission of the program as it furthers the mission of the district as a whole. From that discussion, an overview of the program should emerge based on answers to the following questions:

- What will be the program's primary focus based on the identified needs of the district be?

- At which academic level will the program be implemented?

- What type of students will benefit from enrollment in the program?

- What should the program seek to accomplish in working with these students?

Talk. Think. Talk some more. Rethink. Then reach consensus. For example, would the program exist to support the academic efforts of all secondary students' grades 7-12 or focus, only on grade levels 9 -12? Will special needs students utilize the program as a mainstream setting prior to their re-entry into the larger high school? Will the program serve as a setting in which students with chronic disciplinary issues work to resolve the issues which hinder their academic, personal, and social success? Will the program's primary goal be one of drop-out prevention offering priority placement to those seniors in danger of not graduating? Once the committee of district stakeholders has determined who the program will serve, the next step will be to create a pathway for those possible enrollees to transition from their current school settings into the alternative environment.

How Will Students Be Referred To The Program?
(Pathways Into The Program)

Your counselor recommended you, your parents seem excited
for you; but, if after our discussion, you are not convinced
that this is the place for you, you should not come.

The program's administrator or principal, school counselors, school psychologists, and instructional staff's recommendations may constitute a starting point for identifying prospective students. When I began Center Alternative School in 1989, I served the previous school year as the assistant principal at Center Junior High School. From my contacts with kids in the office that year, I put together a list of students I felt would benefit from an alternative school setting. Based on the four foundation questions, I began talking with students about the possibility of entering the alternative program their freshman year in lieu of attending the traditional high school. Over the course of the year, I had developed strong relationships with both the students and their parents; and we talked a lot about the upcoming school year, their academic and behavioral progress, and our hopes for their educational future.

In preparation for implementing the alternative program, the school counselor and I met frequently to begin identifying specific students with chronic disciplinary problems, attendance issues, poor academic performance, or on-going peer group issues which remained unresolved and consumed a major portion of their school day.

At the high school level referrals to the program came from the counseling department of the sending schools. Each participating high school was allocated a specific number of slots for entry into the program at the beginning of each academic semester. Counselors from the sending schools met together to discuss which of the students on their respective lists would most benefit from enrollment in the alternative program. Once they made their decisions, they contacted the students to let them know that they were on the list to enroll in the alternative program for the upcoming school semester. Their names were given to the alternative program counselor who began to contact students and schedule enrollment interviews to discuss the program and answer any questions they or their parents had regarding the program. Early in my explanation of the program to both students and parents, I made it clear that this was a school of choice. No one could force a student to enter the alternative program. I explained to the parent, that despite the public's often negative perceptions of alternative programs, this was not a place for "bad" kids. The goal of the program was to provide a second chance for those students who for whatever reason, were not experiencing success in their current school setting.

During the enrollment interview, I was very honest with the parents and the students regarding the program's expectations both behaviorally and academically. "Your counselor may have recommended you, and your parents seem excited for you; but, if after our discussion, you are not convinced that this is the place for you, you should not come." The vast majority of parents quickly agreed that the alternative program sounded as though it was tailor-made for their child, and they expressed positive feelings about the potential for their child's success. In the few situations in which the kids and their parents asked for time to think over and digest what we had talked about during the interview, I would tell them that the waiting list was growing, and they needed to make a decision, one way or the other, within the next few days. If the student decided not to attend, I needed to have that information as soon as possible, so I could offer the slot to the next student on the waiting list.

The following criterion was developed to serve as a guide for building counselors as they identified individual students as potential candidates for enrollment in the districts alternative education program:

Student *Choice* in Entering Program

Providing a student with the option to choose his or her educational environment is a powerful motivator. Choice of entry eliminates scapegoating on the part of a student. Individual choice denies the viability of the victim's mentality as a credible defense in the face of personal strife or academic failure. Having made the decision to enter the alternative program, students are now accountable for their own individual success or failure. I told the students, "You chose to become a part of the program you made a commitment to change those things about yourself which resulted in your not being successful in your previous school setting. In doing so, you agreed to do the things necessary for you to walk across the stage with a diploma in your hand. I will hold you to your word."

Need for Modified Curricular Approach

Teacher-initiated adaptations to the district's curriculum enhance individual student strengths, creative abilities, and talents. Many alternative students comment on their teacher's ability to help them understand the assigned material and of the availability of the instructional staff to provide individual assistance as a major strength of alternative educational programs. "The Academy gave me a new outlook on school and an opportunity to succeed when others didn't believe in me. The teachers took their time to make sure I understood the concepts and the lessons being put in front of me, and once I started to understand them, learning became enjoyable." J.C., Senior, 2010. A parent of an Academy student commented, "The teachers know how to teach these kids so they can learn. E. was very unhappy at his huge high school. He is bright but fell between the cracks. When he transferred to the Academy, school became a positive experience again" (Academy Parent Survey, 2002)

Established Patterns of Academic Failure and Non-attendance

For various reasons, students become disenfranchised with the school experience. Such patterns of academic failure and non-attendance often result as a direct consequence of a student experiencing a complete lack of connectedness to his school environment on any personal level. Yet, these patterns can be significantly improved through a student's connection with the teaching staff, the application of flexible scheduling, enrollment in Independent Study classes, and student utilization of available on-line courses.

Diminished Opportunities for School-related Success

The relationships formed by alternative teachers and administrators with their students often serve as an in-road to changing a student's (and often times a family's) negative perceptions of the "school." Sibling drop-out history, the belief that a High School Diploma is not a determinant of future success, or the adverse impact of negative labeling on specific students by teachers and administrators reinforces the students perceptions (and those of his parents) that he is not valued as a student and that his school environment would be better off without him. In conversations with parents regarding the impact of negative labeling on their kids, it was apparent that they believed that school officials reacted in a more aggressive and punitive manner in dealing with their kids behavioral issues than with those students from "good families" who experienced similar behavioral issues. One parent I spoke with during a home visit vented his feelings towards school officials in stating, "They (school officials) ran my older boy out of there, and I'm not going to sit by and watch them do the same thing to this one."

Estranged or Disconnected from Traditional School Setting

Students considering enrollment in an AEP often cite serious, ongoing, peer group conflicts, teen pregnancy, or feelings of being totally disconnected from their school environment as reasons for their transferring to a smaller, more student-centered setting. As A, (2009 graduate), recounts, "Suddenly I felt like an outsider, a nobody, at my home school. I somehow became one of the kids I had once made fun of. But now that it was me, it wasn't funny. I stopped going to school like I was supposed to and began falling behind in my work. Then there was no hope for me, so I simply checked out completely."

Academic Underachiever

One of the most frequent motivators for students seeking admission to an AEP is their refusal to complete and/or hand in assigned homework. The frustration level of their parents is often palpable in response to their child's refusal to complete homework assignments. A typical student response to their failure in a specific class is often expressed as, "I have passed every one of (fill in the teacher's name) exams, I contribute to class discussions on a regular basis, and turn in all my daily assignments. To her, none of this matters. She told me that homework assignments count as 50% of my grade for the class, and then she told me that I couldn't pass her class if I didn't do my homework and turn it in on time." I have found that the majority of students in academic difficulty are there as the direct result of their refusal to do their homework. There's nothing wrong with their brains; they just refuse to play the homework game, and they are willing to fail the class rather than submit to a grade requirement they view as arbitrary on the part of the teacher.

Frequent Contact with the Criminal Justice System

Once in the court system, students are often pegged as trouble with little hope of reform. Yet, in a program that fundamentally focuses on building relationships, even the repeat offenders can find direction. C. a junior coming from California to the plains of Kansas said, "I have been on the other side of the law, and it ended up changing me in a way I would never even imagined. Going through court dates, and probation helped me recognize how the law works. And attending Mr. M's sociology class while going through my personal situation made me realize I can spend the rest of my life as a delinquent, or I can take my experience and become a juvenile attorney helping troubled teenagers work through their troubles and get onto the right path of their lives." In her graduation speech in 2010, C stated, "My high school years have been full of ups and downs, side to sides, but looking back I see my experience at the Academy as a positive one. Here is where I learned who I am, here is where I learned who I want to be, and here is where I learned how I will become the person I now believe I can be."

All prospective enrollees should reflect a majority
of the agreed upon criteria for placement

Individual students seeking entry into the alternative program should experience at least 80% of the agreed on criteria. Furthermore, the sending school counselors and administrators should refer potential students to the program only after the student has indicated a strong interest in attending, and the student's parents have been made aware of their child's desire to enter.

How Will The Program Be Evaluated?
(What will success look like? Expected outcomes)

The potential for individual student success, and by extension, the success of any Alternative Education Program, should be determined as the result of an evaluation process, initiated by the district and based on the criteria established by the district at the program's inception. At the conclusion of each school year the program is in operation, an informal district evaluation involving the program's administrator, its instructional staff, parents, and students should be conducted by district office. One good way is through the use of surveys in which parents evaluate the program's administrator and instructional staff. Additional surveys completed by students provide input regarding specific course content, class structure, teaching styles, individual student learning styles, exam structure, and individual course grade criteria. Interviews conducted by district office officials or their representatives should be conducted with the program's instructional staff, students, and parents, regarding their opinions. Perceptions of the program in general, its impact on their students strengths and weaknesses, and possible changes for the future should be addressed. Information gleaned from interviews and surveys is invaluable in determining which aspects of the program actually work for kids, parents, and staff. Fine tuning the program based on data received from its participants is an ongoing process and should be part and parcel of any end-of-year reflection.

Furthermore, every three years the district should bring in an outside evaluation team, usually from a university or college, to meet with staff, students, parents, and district officials. The team should focus on the program in depth. Such evaluations identify the program's strengths and the areas in which additional thought and attention for the future are needed. Evaluators seek answers to various questions regarding the program's mission from those individuals implementing, supervising, and utilizing the program as its customers.

- Is the program fulfilling its mission?

- Is the program's referral/selection process based on the established criteria?

- Are the program's percentages of special needs students (if applicable), minority students, male to female ratios, and teen parents representative of the populations of the sending schools which it serves?

- What has been the impact of the program on district dropout rates vs. graduation percentage?

- How has assessment score data been collected and in what areas is there demonstrated improvement?

- What is the total number of disciplinary referrals to the office and who wrote them most often? What are the out-of-school suspension percentages vs. other disciplinary approaches (restitution, ISS, administration conference, counselor referral, etc.)?

- How are potential students informed of the program in their parent schools?

- If a student is interested, did the parent school counselor contact the student's parents and arrange a meeting to discuss the benefits of enrolling their son or daughter in the program?

- Has the program met or exceeded the districts agreed upon criteria for success?

End of year evaluations of the program are essential for the health of the program. Data analysis provides the program with the flexibility to sharpen its focus, to adapt, and to grow based on the needs of the population it serves. End of year evaluations a side, no matter how successful a district deems its AEP, it's the public's perceptions of the program which will determine its longevity or lack of it within any given district. Board members come and go, as do superintendents. School district's with long standing AEP's, have successfully promoted the program's successes within the community and continue to do so year in and year out.

How will the district introduce and promote the program within the community?

You can invest in a kid now and send them to Penn State; or you can refuse to do so and send them to the state pen.

The first order of business after being hired as the AEP's principal is to schedule as many meetings as possible with local civic organizations. The goal is to provide their members with a general overview of the program. Over the summer months, long before the doors open to the first student, contact every civic organization in the community and volunteer to be their guest speaker at their regular meeting. On most occasions ask for about twenty minutes to introduce yourself and your program to the assembled group. Have a specific idea of what you want to say and make the presentation as engaging as possible. Answer all their questions to the best of your ability, be positive, and ask for community assistance in the form of volunteers, scholarships, and mentors to assist staff in the core curriculum areas. Invite the organization's membership to visit the building and attempt to build a relationship with any organization showing an interest in interacting with the program. In making introductions, I have utilized a little street theatre, making my presentation as personal and dramatic as I could, so that those individuals attending the meeting would remember what I said, talk about what I said to others in the community, and leave the meeting thinking that they have become my partner in doing "*God's*" work. In closing, stress to the audience that education is an investment in human potential, and that the school district, in deciding to implement an Alternative Education Program, is making a commitment to those students for whom the public school setting is synonymous with personal and academic failure. Rather than accept the fact these kids failed and just throw them away, the district is providing a pathway for these students to succeed.

Contact the local newspaper and speak to someone regarding the program and the plans for the upcoming school year. Talk with business owners located in close proximity to the building. Get to know them by name. Invite kids to the building to plant trees, paint walls, and help get the building ready for the first day of school. Provide lunch, hang out with them, and begin to build relationships. Be at the school every day and welcome those students who come by. Talk with the juvenile officer and the local police. Get to know them and let them know that they are welcome any time. Walk the town square at lunch, eat in the local café, be visible, be open, and be willing to spend time talking with people about what the school hopes to accomplish in the upcoming year. Do the little things that make people in the community feel comfortable and make them willing to come by and discuss negative rumors they have heard about what goes on in the program, before they blindly pass on these rumors.

Any new education program introduced into a community will have its detractors. Unfounded negative rumors regarding the program will persist even in the face of common sense. An example occurred one morning when a district patron entered our building and announced that she was here to "find the smoking room". Her daughter had just been suspended from the traditional school for smoking, and she was upset that kids in the Alternative Program were allowed to smoke without any consequences. She was angry. I asked her to come and find me when she found the room and went about my business. She looked around the school and left without another word. No such room existed, but she had heard that it did. Work to dispel negative rumors, be patient, be courteous, listen, and always promote the need for the community to support kids regardless of established stereotypes.

There is an old saying among alternative teachers and principals "that you can invest in a kid now and send them to Penn State or you can refuse to do so and send them to the State Pen. You will eventually pay for them one way or the other." As an AEP principal opening a new program, a million things have to be done before welcoming kids on their first day of school. Focus energy on making sure the building is ready for kids, but never lose sight of how important it is to maintain a connection with the community — if the goal is to welcome students on the first day of the program's *second year*.

CHAPTER 2

Criteria for Implementation

Any school district serious about designing and implementing an Alternative Education Program needs to provide the community an opportunity to meet, comment, discuss, and explore all educational options relating to its implementation. In doing so, all district stakeholders need to be involved in the process.

Selecting and Organizing a Committee

A district's organizational committee may include district office administration, secondary building principals, counselors, district social workers/psychologists, representatives from the business community, Juvenile Justice (Probation Officers), district patrons, teachers, parents and students. I know it sounds like a lot of people, but all have a valid reason for participating and should have the opportunity to do so. Once a committee is formed, schedule visits for the committee to surrounding districts which already have alternative programs already up and running. Have them spend the day talking with teachers, students, office staff, and the program's administrators. Have a list of questions prepared and ask them. Schedule a time for the committee to meet and discuss what they learned from their visits. What worked well in the program? What things seemed a little out of whack? What was the overall tone and feel of the building? What were they doing in terms of building policies, disciplinary strategies, referral processes;

daily schedules, instructional approaches, and curriculum which might be a good fit for your program?

Send district representatives to Alternative/At-Risk conferences to listen and talk with experts in the field. Be honest in explaining to them where the district is in terms of implementation of a program and ask questions. Research data, read articles, gather all the available information. Then, meet and begin answering the foundation questions based on the individual district's needs. Once those questions have answers and a framework is built from which to work, begin the discussion of how the program will be funded and where it will be housed within the district.

Site Selection

Location is really just a state of mind in which the concept of a school grows. Classrooms in long abandoned elementary buildings, store fronts off the square in a rural community, an unused classroom, a district storage facility converted into four classrooms — all of these have served as the initial location for programs I've started over the past 30 years. I've found almost any available space will do when beginning an Alternative Education Program. The Butler Alternative School began in an old appliance store just off of the town square. Portable walls were constructed on wheels creating classroom space, dividing space in the large open front of the building; and then moved the walls to the sides to provide a common lunchroom for kids and staff to eat. Space was minimal and the number of kids enrolled did not exceed twenty-five. The building had serious structural defects, only one unisex bathroom, no storage or locker area for students to use; but as the year progressed, our kids and staff accepted it as their own. Our building was often cold in the winter, and frequently smelled strongly of sewer gas, but it came to be our space.

The staff brought in electric skillets and cooked a hot breakfast for our kids every Friday morning. Our gym was a nearby park. Forty degrees or above and no wind became the standard for shortening classes and spending time playing football or basketball in the park. The public library served as our research lab and supported our reading program. Due to our location, we were very visible to the community, and as a result, we reminded our kids everyday about public perceptions of our program, and how important it was that as a school, we never gave anyone in the community a reason to be involved with us in a negative way.

After lunch each day, those students in good standing could walk with our staff to a grocery store located on the corner of the town square. It was a risk for our program. If any of our kids did anything stupid along the way, such as ducking out for a quick smoke, or were loud, or their behavior viewed as inappropriate by patrons, I would hear about it from the superintendent. We walked to the store at the same time every day and people would sometimes come out of their stores and talk with our kids and teachers. Mostly, they just watched from their windows as we passed by. When I would go into a local business on the square, the person who waited on me would always about the program and comment about seeing us everyday walking to and from the corner store. At large group meetings I stressed the importance of building good will in the community. I wanted our kids to understand that their public behaviors, whether positive or negative, would make or break the public's perception of the program. When kids violated school rules, I assigned them restitution around the building: Washing windows, sweeping the front sidewalk, or picking up trash on the street outside our building. I notified the local paper of our scheduled building and street cleanup days. The local paper supported our efforts within the community by publishing positive articles about our program, interviewing students, and taking photographs of our kids and staff in action.

Over the summer the district completed work on our new building, and we moved into a new facility to begin our second year. Our program finally had a home with real classrooms, indoor gym, adequate restrooms, hallways lined with lockers, and our own kitchen and commons area. As our kids came by to visit their new building prior to the first day of school, they walked the halls, checked out the bathrooms, scoped out where they wanted their locker, and hung out in the commons. From their excited chatter as they talked with staff and roamed the building, it was evident that they felt at home.

In choosing the initial site for implementation of the districts alternative education program remember that kids need a place to connect, and staff needs a place to work. The location is really a state of mind in which the concept of a program grows and is nurtured by those who work and attend there. A program's initial space doesn't have to be pretty; it does have to have plumbing, heat, and be a place where kids come first.

Funding Your Program

A stable and continuous district plan for funding your program is vital if the program is to have the time necessary to establish itself in the hearts and minds of the community which it serves. Unfortunately, in many districts, AEP's without a stable source of funding are first to be discontinued when district budgets become tight. Funding for the majority of Alternative Educational Programs originates from the state, through decreasing yearly grants or distribution of At-Risk monies. A minority of programs are funded from the originating district's general fund. Program allocations from the district may be based on yearly enrollment numbers, projected operating costs, and the number of instructional staff assigned to the program. A small percentage of programs are based on the cooperative model in which surrounding districts agree to pool their resources and students in support of a program. The larger, more centrally located district usually hosts the site with each participating district providing tuition and transportation for its students. Material support in the form of individual student records, IEP's, and transcript maintenance is provided by the cooperating districts which retain their kids on their school's roster.

Experienced alternative teachers and administrators know that they must never depend on their district to give them what they need to do their jobs; they must provide for themselves. As a staff we became very good at scrounging for furniture and additional resource and classroom materials. The bottom line for any alternative program is that its funding sources must be sustainable year in and year out if the program is to remain a stable and viable educational option for students and their families.

Staff Selection

Once the district is committed to the implementation of an Alternative program, staff selection becomes the primary focus of both district office and the program's principal. This is the tricky part. Not every teacher perceives the chance to teach in an Alternative program as an opportunity worth pursuing. At a district meeting a traditional teacher made the comment to our CA teacher that she was wasting her talents in choosing to teach in the district's alternative program. For a minority of your district's instructional staff, however, it's what they've been waiting for their entire careers. Yet, those few who embrace the challenge often find themselves on the receiving end of student criticisms when discussing their students previous contacts and experiences with classroom teachers. As an alternative classroom teacher for over three decades, I quickly discovered that I could throw out everything I had learned in my education method's classes. The primary mission is to build relationships with the kids. Building and sustaining relationships is the key to success with at-risk kids. In the absence of strong, positive-based relationships, teachers become just another person telling students to do something they don't want to do. Without strong relationships, students feel the teacher has no value, does not understand them, and are unwilling to make any effort to do so. The message to potential staff is clear: You must become the reason a kid decides to change those things about him or herself that have not worked for them in the past with regard to the school setting.

Old habits, old roles are hard to put aside, whether you are a student or an educator. The staff must become the catalyst for change. The ability to build relationships with kids is as important to the program as the staff's individual expertise in their respective subject areas. On days when one of my teachers would come into my office after school frustrated, upset, and looking for help, I would listen, ask questions, offer encouragement; and then, I reminded them "if it were easy anyone could do it."

As a teacher, forget about where students should be in terms of content at a specific time, or about grades, or meeting district standards on assessments. Once you've established that you'll be there every day, that your expectations for behavior will be enforced, and you have fought and won the early battles, you can begin to introduce the curriculum in a more consistent manner. Now, you will be doing so to an audience whose perceptions of the power of knowledge have changed.

A., a 2010 graduate, shared the following with the audience of board members, family, community advocates at her graduation ceremony:

"Since I've been at the Academy, I have literally felt my brain grow bigger and bigger. My thoughts and opinions have developed enormously, and I owe a huge thank you to all of the teachers who have been willing to share as well as listen. My desire to learn and grow intellectually has increased the value in my life." To that, I add, "Say it with me brothers and sisters; knowledge is power. Get some."

I recommend to all Alternative principals that the first teacher they hire be themselves. Other candidates for instructional positions should possess the following attributes:

- **Highly qualified** (degree in the subject matter area they are hired to teach)

- **The ability to adapt curriculum to the varying ability levels of their students** (not all students have to move at the same pace or in the same manner as long as they are able to demonstrate mastery of the material taught in some agreed on manner.)

- **Choice of setting.** Just as students attend by choice, teachers should apply by choice. (Unfortunately, many districts staff their Alternative programs based on a "tour of duty" mentality - teachers are assigned to the alternative school for a semester and then return to their parent school. Other districts utilize their Alternative programs as a means to remove or retire tenured staff members they feel should no longer be in a classroom. Just as choice of entry is an important aspect relating to a student's success in an Alternative program, instructional staff must also choose to become part of any successful Alternative Education Program. Alternative instructional staff are charged with the dual mission of ensuring that their students meet the academic requirements necessary for graduation while creating an environment in which students can overcome previous barriers to their success. They have to care more than anyone else about their kids' well-being, accept no excuses for any effort less than their students best, and expect their students to achieve both personal and academic success.)

During the enrollment interview I explained to all prospective enrollees that the teachers they will encounter here are very different from any they have experienced in their previous educational settings. "Teachers are here because they want to be, not because they have been assigned here. They will bend over backwards to help you succeed as long as you are willing to help yourself. They will treat you with respect and dignity with the expectation that you will treat them likewise."

- **The ability to build strong positive relationships with students, resulting in the teacher achieving "significant other" status in the eyes of their students.** Relationships between a student and teacher serve as the framework for real change to occur regarding a student's effort in the classroom and a willingness for the student to take the necessary risks to overcome previous school related (negative) behaviors. In my experience, it usually takes a semester for at-risk students to shed their old roles regarding their school environment and adjust to the expectations and norms governing their new setting. The goal is to help the students view themselves as part of something positive. Many students enter Alternative programs never really thinking that they will graduate. Once they are embraced by a caring, dedicated, and demanding staff, they not only see graduation as probable, but they also see college and a career as a reality. Alternative teachers become the catalysts for change within a student's thinking, perceptions, and plans after graduation. Once a student has internalized the expectations of staff and the norms of the program, he/she begins to blossom both as a student and as human being. Students begin to relax, to smile more, and to focus on achieving success in their classrooms. Subconsciously, they begin to transfer those same feelings of success to other aspects of their lives away from school.

"My first week at the Academy provided me with a complete change of heart. I wasn't alone … I never knew a school where I felt important just by being there. Every day I walk into school I'm greeted with a smile by my teachers and principal. In class, if I am having a problem, my teacher works with me individually; and since the class sizes are smaller, she can show every single student the same consideration. Our teachers understand we're individuals, and as such, we have unique individual requirements for learning from a standard pupil. We're not spoiled; we didn't volunteer to be

completely divergent and have the special needs that we do we just are. And while my home school alienated me for that and made the issues worse, the teachers at the Academy have not only acknowledged our individuality but completely embraced them (A. D., Student Essay, 2009)

In our program, academic progress reports went home every three weeks whether the student had an A or an F. Making the honor roll became a big deal. Students took their certificates home and later told me that their parents put them on the refrigerator. Many kids said this was the first time they had made the honor roll since the sixth grade. Once on the honor role, maintaining a high grade point average became an important goal for the majority of students. We built an incentive to help support them maintain their new found success. If a student had a B in every class and had missed ten days or fewer or been tardy to school ten times or less in any academic semester, they were excused from taking final exams. Meeting this criteria meant eligible students would end their academic semester four days earlier than everyone else. This simple proposal became a powerful incentive for our students to make their grades, get to school on time, honor their commitment to the program, and build their individual self-esteem along the way.

- **Possess the missionary zeal regarding alternative kids and their families.** "Your job may be to teach in the program, but your mission is to make a positive difference in a kid's life each and every day."

"The teachers and staff are the best! They know that these kids are going to challenge them and they are up for it. The teachers care about each child and the kids know it" (BVA Parent Survey, 2002).

"The Blue Valley Academy is rarely spoken of in a flattering manner. Alternative students are often misconstrued as anti-social, indolent losers, who couldn't make it in regular school. And although students here may not flaunt a 4.0 GPA and may not participate in every after school activity or paint our faces for every home game, we are still human. We feel defeat when life hands us lemons; we mess up; and we fall down...just like you. And while many people don't realize this, one doesn't have to be a cookie cutter, angel student to argue truth. And the truth is, as undermined as alternative education's reputation get...the Academy has saved our lives" (A.D., Student Essay, 2009).

- **Dedication to their chosen profession.** As principal of an Alternative high School, I was often invited to speak to groups of education students ready to begin their student teaching experience. I would begin our discussion with a simple statement, "Your commitment to your kids and their families takes precedent over everything else in your school environment." During the next eight weeks, I would encourage each of them to become visible, open, and accessible to their students on a daily basis; to immerse themselves in the culture of their school, to begin building the foundations necessary for them to become effective classroom teachers, and to become a force for good in their school. "You'll be busy, you'll work harder than you've ever worked before, you'll be pressed for time, and you'll never feel as though you're as prepared as you should be for Monday. But never lose sight of the reason you decided to become a teacher in the first place. Teaching is not about which committee you sit on, or to which professional organization you belong, or in gaining tenure. Teaching is about service, and mission, and commitment to your kids who need and depend on you to be your very best every day."

A Brief Respite

After writing that last line I suddenly thought of my youngest daughter who is beginning her fourth year as an elementary teacher in the Chicago Public School System. Emily is a force to be reckoned with in her classroom. "Ms. Gann don't play" was the student line on her from her split class of fifth and sixth graders. She can be steely at times. She has struggled with the politics of a large, urban system, overcrowded classrooms (she once had thirty-seven kindergarteners without a full time aide), unscrupulous administrators, and a hierarchy of long term staff who long ago lost whatever it was that made them want to become teachers in the first place. When I listen to her stories, I can hear her love for her kids, and her frustrations with an entrenched system and the people who wrap themselves in its protective tentacles. She has the convictions of an evangelist bent on saving those who will not lift a finger to save themselves. She also has the energy, creativeness, and tenacity to question those things about her school that she feels are not in the best interests of her kids or her profession. She and many of her colleagues teaching in urban classrooms, represent a teaching corps less interested in the politics of advancement than in doing what is best (and needed) for their students to succeed both in school and in the tough neighborhoods they return to every evening.

Continuation of instructional attributes...

- **A willingness to think outside the box. Be solution oriented, performance based, and student centered in your approach to kids.** Kids want connections with adults with whom they can communicate and feel comfortable. Kids will naturally gravitate towards members of the staff who embody those characteristics in their approach to them. Building relationships with kids will pay dividends when things go south, as they occasionally do with at-risk kids. Having a basis for communication with both the student and their families will allow for an honest and straight forward approach in addressing disciplinary problems when they arise. Parents will support an administrator or teacher they believe is supportive of their student, understands their student's issues, and are acting in the best interest of their student.

"Our son would not have graduated from high school if not for the innovative teaching methods of the Academy and the insightful and caring teachers. The Academy allowed our son to experience success in completing class requirements for the first time in his high school career. The Academy helped him to realize his potential! Thank you!" (BVA Parent Survey, 2002).

"Almost every student who walks these halls has experienced a raw and uncensored view of life and although that may make us appear harder, more rebellious, or even hopeless to an ignorant world, we simply needed someone to understand and help us get back on track. Like the school's mascot, The Phoenix, we have risen from the ashes of trials that most people...won't face in a lifetime. This is a school of fighters, an ongoing story of personal triumph, and a portrait of living proof that character, success, and life itself can be rebuilt from the vestiges of a failed past... The Academy provides its students with a once-in-a-lifetime chance to be born again...Instead of giving up on us in the most crucial point of our lives, this school has provided

us with not only a high school education, but also a set of life skills, a sense of community, and an understanding that even when your back is against the wall, there is hope…" (A. D., Student Essay, 2009).

- **Possess effective communication skills.** (All Alternative staff members act as informal counselors, advisors, and listeners.)

Improved attendance, improved attitudes, improved grades, and an appreciation for the effort it took to make those grades, are all by-products of a kid altering his perceptions of his school environment and of him re-defining his role within that environment.

CHAPTER 3

Components of a True Alternative Educational Program

*A student's impressions of his or her learning environment are
critical to the student's concept of educational relevance.*

All alternative education programs share similar characteristics (at least
the successful ones.) It's not about reinventing the wheel; it's about
meeting the needs of individual students in a meaningful and effective
manner. This chapter will explore the philosophical components of
a true, student-centered, performance-based Alternative Education
Program.

Choice of Entry

Choice of entry is a powerful motivator. It eliminates scapegoating
on the part of the student and is the first step in the student shedding
the victim's mentality. Parents are often enthusiastic at the possibility
of their student attending an Alternative program. They view their
student's enrollment as an opportunity for them to succeed at school,
perhaps turn things around at home, grow up a bit, and finally get
back on track toward graduation. No matter how excited a parent
is regarding the program, however; if the student has no interest, he
should not be enrolled. The student must have a stake in his own
success. In my experience, students who invest in their school will

tend to cooperate with, rather than disrupt, a learning environment which meets their needs. Student choice with regard to enrollment in an Alternative Educational Program fosters the acceptance of personal responsibility for individual behavior, and reduces both student and parental dissatisfaction with unwanted or undesirable educational mandates imposed by the traditional school.

A school setting, which encourages individual students to actively share in the educational decisions which impact their lives, offers the student practical experience in decision making, long term planning, and the experience of individual accomplishment. Furthermore, the student feels the personal satisfaction in completing their educational plan, as well as examining the potential negative consequences should he fail to maintain his commitment to himself and to his school. In short, when students have a vested interest in their school environment, they are more likely to view their school as a place where they feel accepted and valued. Ensuring the option of choice, with regard to an individual's educational setting, greatly enhances the likelihood that potential dropouts or those who have already left the public school environment will return to and/or remain in the educational environment. In short, students will stay in a program in which they have a voice in determining their educational plan.

The Enrollment Interview

At the enrollment interview, I make it clear to both student and parents that the student's decision to attend the Alternative school begins a new chapter in the student's life. I tell them choosing to attend can lead the student towards making better decisions, building internal controls, growing up a little, and walking across the stage with a diploma in hand. I let both student and parents know that what happened in the past regarding their student's academic performance or behavior does not matter here. When they chose to enroll in the Academy, they make a commitment to do the things necessary to succeed as a person and as a student which will result in a graduation celebration. During the interview, I take a moment to let both parties know the Alternative program is also making a commitment to their student by providing a safe, secure, and supportive environment in which the student can take advantage of the second chance opportunity.

This is often the first face-to-face contact between the referred student, parents, and the program's administrator. The initial meeting should be viewed by the program's administrator as the first opportunity to begin building positive relationships with both the student and parents. I always began the interview by asking; "What have you heard about the Academy?" Their initial response will dictate the course of the conversation. I did my best to dispel any negative rumors, if mentioned, and stress the program's focus on being student-centered and performance-based, both academically and behaviorally. I explained the importance of regular school attendance and the expectation of graduation for every student as a goal of the program. I let both parents and student know it didn't matter what happened to them at their previous school. I told students the past is the past and not important here. "No one is going to read your record, nobody cares what you did or didn't do in your previous school setting. What does matter is what you intend to do with a second chance to succeed and graduate from high school."

Early in the interview I always asked the student if he had a picture in his head of walking across the stage with a diploma in his hand. If the answer was "no," I asked him to contact me when he was ready to do the things necessary to graduate. If the answer to that question was "yes," we began to build a plan to make that happen.

Interview Format

- Ask for questions or concerns
- Review the student's current academic transcript
- Lay out a plan for credit recovery and graduation
- Discuss further questions or concerns
- Explain the attendance/academic policies
- Get a commitment from the student
- Get a commitment from the parents

After the initial discussion, I took the time to ask both the parents and the student if they had any questions or concerns. As we began to talk about the student's current academic transcript; Dr. H would tally the number of student's credits earned to date and lay out a plan for the student to earn the additional credits necessary to for graduation. Together we began to build the bridge from where the student was that day to where the student wanted to be at this time next year. After this, we would discuss any questions or concerns the parents or the student had regarding his educational plan. I explained the attendance/academic policies, the big four rules which comprise the foundation of the program's disciplinary policies, and stressed the program's expectation that all students will honor their commitment to do the things necessary to graduate. I worked to get a commitment from the student to change those things about himself that didn't work well in the past. I also got a commitment from the parent to support the program and their student in meeting the expectations while attending with the end goal of graduation.

Let the parents know that the staff will act as an advocate for their student and that the staff and administration will provide a safe and secure environment in which their student can thrive and succeed. Remind the parents they are always welcome at school should they have questions or concerns and that the staff will communicate with them on a frequent basis regarding their student's academic progress. Finally, stress that the staff and administration will do their best to ensure individual student success, *as long as the student is willing to help himself.*

Student Commitment

School administrators cannot sentence a student to an alternative education environment and expect any real change in attitude, academic achievement, or commitment on the part of the student. Students entering the Alternative program must internalize the commitment necessary to risk real change in their approach to their school environment and make the effort necessary to succeed when faced with adversity.

Every student enters the program with an established set of beliefs and practices in response to the demands of school. For at-risk kids, those behaviors may include academic failure, truancy, behavioral issues, school phobias, and substance abuse issues. The list of why they haven't succeeded in the past is endless; and more often than not, the lack of educational success, according to the student and often the parent, is a direct result of their previous school's teachers, cliques, peer groups, and principal's behavior towards them. One goal of the initial interview is to communicate all staff, students, and administrators are responsible for what they do, what they say, and how they behave. Each of these impacts those around them. Stress to the student that you are available; and that if anything should happen, he should come and find you to let you know what's going on. "Don't wait until the issue has become so serious that it interferes with your ability to do your job at school, and you feel that you have no options. Everyone has bad days; all of us make mistakes, both adults and kids." The goal is to assist students in finding ways to break their cycle of negative behaviors associated with school. The underlying goal is to help kids learn from their mistakes, and not continue to make the same ones over and over.

Assure the parents that should their student decide to come to the alternative school that all the staff will work with their son or daughter to resolve any issues which arise. "This is a place where kids can learn to make better choices for themselves, grow up a little, get back on track academically, and graduate." Be polite, be supportive, but never deviate from the message that the student is in charge of his own success or failure. Alternative teachers/administrators are facilitators. They are not responsible for the success or failure of individual students. Their job is to provide the student with options leading to personal, social, and academic success. Remind parents, "You are always welcome at school, you don't need an appointment if you have concerns or questions. Call me or come by should you need to do so." Shake their hands, thank them for coming in, and remind the student of the first day of school and of their commitment to walk through the front doors on the first day, ready to take care of business. Smile and welcome both parent and student to their new school.

Representative of the District it Serves

In developing the district's criteria for placement, it is important for the sending school counselors and administrators to support and maintain fair and consistent placement guidelines. Failure to do so often results in the Alternative program becoming identified as a place where students of color, those exhibiting the most severe behavioral issues, substance abuse, criminal activity, or unexpected pregnancy attend.

The rule of thumb in determining which students attend the district's Alternative program is based on the premise that the program's population closely mirrors that of its sending schools. For example, if the district's minority population is five per cent and the Alternative programs minority enrollment is double or triple that number, then the sending school's system for identifying specific students for referral to the Alternative program is seriously flawed. The same holds true with male to female ratio, the number of special needs students, or teen parents. Of course, those kids will show up. Your job is to instill in each of them the philosophy of living in a fish bowl. Anything they do at school or in the community that can be construed as negative will be embraced by skeptics in the community and used as proof that the program is not a place where decent kids attend. I explain to kids that when negative things do happen in the community (unstructured time over spring break or Christmas can be challenging for at-risk kids and their parents) the focus is always on the impact of their behavior on the reputation of their school. I tell them that their choices, their behaviors, when perceived as negative by those in the community, only serve to perpetuate the stereotypes associated with an Alternative program. People are far more willing to believe the worst rather than communicate the positive. The student population, therefore, should reflect the sending school's community to avoid the alternative school being perceived as a dumping ground for the district's least desirable students.

Prospective students are placed on a priority list developed by their home-school counselors and submitted to the Alternative program's counselor at the end of each academic semester. Parents are then contacted by the program's counselor or principal and scheduled for an interview. Parent-school counselors are encouraged to be familiar enough with the Alternative program that they can answer specific questions regarding the program, provide a general overview, and explain the program's relationship with the sending schools.

As the principal of an Alternative Education Program, do your best to adhere to the established placement criteria, even in the face of pressure from the traditional school administrators. At times, some may request the immediate placement of a student, at a time other than the established criteria which should be at the beginning of the next academic semester. When listening to all of the reasons for exempting the agreed upon placement criteria, including, "If you don't accept this student now, she will more than likely dropout of school," — stick to the agreed upon plan. Don't give in to emotion. If you still don't commit, they may simply go over your head to your supervisor. On more than one occasion, a sending school administrator stated to me that he knew I would say no to his request to place a student immediately. He wanted me to know that he was prepared to go over my head regarding the matter. When that happened, I attended the meeting and made my case, agreeing to abide by my supervisor's decision. You'll win some and lose some, *but never compromise by making it easy for sending school administrators to manipulate the agreed upon placement criteria and threaten the integrity of your program.*

Non-punitive By Design

Punishment is a prerogative of the judiciary, not an educational tool.

I learned early on that it is far more important for a kid to behave responsibly than obediently (See Chapter 4 on "Positive Based Disciplinary Practices"). As a classroom teacher or building principal, one can never punish a kid enough to make him want to learn, or change, or do anything he doesn't want to do in relation to his school environment. The typical at-risk student is not going to earn his or her way back into the traditional school setting, as some administrators believe. If he wanted to remain in that environment, he would still be there. Discipline should be progressive, reasonable, fair, and consistent. Keep your list of rules short, but be very direct about their enforcement and don't let anything slide.

For example, assigned restitution in response to a student's use of inappropriate language, tobacco violations, truancy, and general misconduct is an effective way in which students are made aware of their behavior and your expectation that they find another way in which to express themselves, curb their addictions, commit to regular attendance, and manage their own behaviors. I would remind the offending student, as a part of the Alternative program, he or she bore a special burden to always act in the best interest of the school. I would tell students they did not have to live their labels. I challenged them to defy expectations and succeed. I ask, "Why give anyone a reason to be involved with you (us) in a negative way. Be aware of your environment, watch your language, your behaviors, and use your powers (talents) for good not evil." When students committed an offense, and in doing so, embarrassed their school, I gave them the "special responsibility speech" before assigning restitution or escorting them off our campus to begin their suspensions.

Assigning restitution in the form of washing lunch tables in the commons, doing dishes, picking up trash around the building, and sweeping the gym floor is preferable to assigning out-of-school suspension. Out-of-school suspension should only be used when the student gives you no other option, and you feel it's necessary for them to take a few days to re-establish their perspective regarding their role in the program. "Take two days and think about what it is you really want regarding school. If you come back on Tuesday, it's with the understanding that you're going to do whatever you're asked to do, when you're asked to do it. If I don't see you on Tuesday, I'll understand you've made other educational plans for the reminder of the semester."

It's all about commitment to success. Invest in the chronic offenders; support them when given the opportunity; hold them accountable for their behavior; and continue to expect that they can and will make better choices for themselves. It usually takes one semester for new students to adjust to the expectations of staff and administration. Many students blossom earlier; but for some, it's a question of role behaviors which are deeply entrenched and comfortable, and which have served as the foundation of game-playing techniques, at which at-risk kids are masters. Change students perspective of their role in the school, of how they see themselves in relation to others in the school, and they begin to take care of themselves.

Furthermore, students who feel connected to their educational environment and its staff are less likely to engage in behaviors which violate the norms of their school. For example, in the first nine weeks of the 2008-09 school year, we had 43 office referrals. In the second nine weeks we had 36. The program enrolled 27 new students at winter break. The third nine weeks we had 26 office referrals, the fourth nine weeks only 16. Our veteran students began to internalize their commitment to the program and police themselves. They had also become advisors to those students newly enrolled. Having students take an active role in maintaining the expectations of the program is a good and positive thing to behold. The major result — a decrease in time, energy, and resources staff must commit to enforce the program's behavioral expectations. Generally, a quick word in the hallway between classes or while walking down to breakfast is sufficient to resolve or to head-off an impending situation. Stress with the instructional staff the benefits of building relationships with their kids. Teachers, whose approach in dealing with student disciplinary issues are solution-oriented rather than punitive, are more likely to decrease the amount of time spent on student discipline during the course of a class period, and are more effective in resolving issues which do arise.

Environment In Support of Real Academic, Personal, and Social Change

Alternative Educational Programs must convey a simple message to both students and their parents: This is a place where you can begin again.

Alternative schools must convey a simple message to both students and their parents. This is a place where they can begin again. The underlying message to students is to shed their pasts, shed their victim's mentality, and begin to seek success as a daily goal. Create an atmosphere within the building where real change can become a reality supported by a staff that truly wants to be involved with kids, understands their need for support and structure, and is willing to invest in kids day in and day out. Scrounge some old furniture, get some plants, create spaces throughout the building where kids can gather and talk between classes and over lunch. Start the day interacting with every student who walks through the door, "Good morning, welcome to Tuesday." Talk with kids about things other than school. Once a level of trust is built, they will begin to talk about their issues, their concerns, their parents, their impending court date, what happened to them or their friends in the community over the weekend, etc. A student facing an uncertain fate in court is a good example. "If you survive your court date this afternoon, remember to consider another chance as an opportunity to prove to those people that they no longer need to be involved with you. If you don't give them a reason to continue their involvement with you, they will focus on someone else. Just put this nonsense behind you and get on with the business of getting an education."

As most alternative teachers and administrators will attest, once their kids have a relationship with them and begin to trust them, they will begin to share things about themselves, their families, and their personal relationships. Once that line has been crossed, knowledge of a situation and of a student's involvement cannot be ignored. I ask students, "What do you want me to do about what you've just shared with me?" My focus in this conversation would be to discuss options available to the student. If the student feels capable of implementing one of the options, we discuss the plan or seek the intervention of a trusted family member. I would also ask permission to discuss the situation with our counselor in order to expand the number of options available. I would encourage the student to share the information with our counselor, as she may have other information which may improve the immediate situation. If the student stated he needed more time to find a solution, I would agree to the request with the understanding if he/ she came to me again with this issue and I felt they were being harmed or exploited in some manner, I would intervene regardless of who may be involved.

When these situations occurred, I often went to our counselor for advice and counsel. She would listen and then give her opinion regarding the matter. Before I left her office we would agree on a plan of action the purpose of which would hopefully support the needs of our student while working towards a resolution of the situation.

An equally important consideration would be for the two of us to avoid the possibility of getting sued or being sent to jail. The alternative maxim of always acting in the best interests of the students was often tested when faced with a situation in which our actions may result in unintended negative consequences for the individuals involved. One such instance occurred when C came into my office and asked if she could speak to me. I asked her if this was a general conversation or one which required me to shut my door. She indicated that it was a private matter. When I asked her what was going on, she told me she was pregnant and had scheduled an appointment for an abortion early next week. When I asked her if she had been to a doctor to confirm her pregnancy, she stated she had. I also asked her if she had seriously considered her decision to seek an abortion, and did she need to speak with our counselor or our nurse? She stated that she had already made up her mind and began to explain that her older sister had also become pregnant during her junior year. She informed me her sister had made the mistake of telling her mom about her condition. Her mom's response was to remove her sister from school and send her to her grandmother's home until she delivered her baby, refusing to consider any option other than her sister keeping and raising her child, despite her sister's feelings that she was incapable. She told me that should her mother become aware of her condition, she was afraid her mom would do the same thing to her. She had made a mistake, but she didn't feel her future should be a repeat of her older sister's or have to be constantly reminded by her family of her indiscretion and the results of her poor choices. The student had decided not to inform either her family or the baby's father and just take care of her situation on her own. I asked her why she had decided to tell me of her decision. Her response was that she trusted me and needed to talk with someone about her decision who would not judge her. I explained to her that by her telling me of her decision, she had placed me in a very difficult situation. I explained the concept of the mandatory reporter, which by law required me to notify her parents of her impending decision. If I didn't notify her parents and something bad happened, as the result of her having the procedure, and it became known I had prior knowledge of what she intended to do and I told no one, "All hell would break loose" She became angry with me; and told me if I notified her mom, I would be ensuring that her future was over. She left my office angry and upset. I immediately sought out our counselor, told her what had happened, and asked her opinion about what we should do regarding the information the student had just shared with me. The counselor saw no alternative to informing the student's parents, but suggested that I talk with her and give her a time frame in which to inform her parents of her condition. Should we not hear from her mom regarding that discussion by a specific date, we would have no choice but to notify her parents regardless of her wishes in the matter. I also informed our nurse of the student's condition and of her decision to seek an abortion in the very near future. Both our counselor and our nurse spoke with the student as a result of my having discussed her situation with them. She was very upset at my lack of secrecy and told me so in no uncertain terms. Our relationship was destroyed in the process. She did notify her parents of her condition, and their response was just as she had feared. Her parents removed her from our program and I never saw or heard from her again. As a staff we had done the right thing, but the raw emotion of betrayal she expressed to me stayed with me for a long time.

Students and parents should walk into the building or classroom and get a sense that this place is somehow different from their previous school environment. Alternative teachers and principals have to care more than anyone else, at a level of caring which permeates every conversation, every interaction, and every action. Positive-based, student-teacher relationships are most frequently mentioned by both parents and students enrolled in Alternative Education programs as a major strength of the program.

I just wanted to let you know how pleased I am to see the change in my son's attitude about school since attending the academy. He seems very happy with his decision to change schools, and he seems encouraged about the year ahead. Just last night he told me 'Mom, if all teachers cared about kids as much as mine do, all schools would be better' (BVA parent, August, 2008).

Be open, be supportive, and let students know on a regular basis when they have stepped over the line, or begun to turn the corner in terms of behavior and academic effort. Explain the situation, propose a solution, and get students to acknowledge why a staff member or peer may be upset with them, their behavior, or their words. The message to an offending student is clear, "Today you made poor choices in response to the situation in which you found yourself, but tomorrow is another day." Review expectations for the student regarding their behavior beginning tomorrow. Get the student to give her word that she will make an effort to resolve the situation. Be flexible in your approach, stay on message, keep your word and expect no less from the students in your program. Stress communication *not confrontation* in interactions with both parents and students. Explain your actions and your reasoning for them, but never lose sight of your goal to help students learn to manage their own personal behavior.

Not Terminal by Design

Alternative Educational Programs should not be dead ends for those students enrolled. In designing a program stress the need for continued contact between students and their sending school. The program is structured so that classes begin at 9 a.m. daily. Students needing to enroll in courses not offered by the Alternative program could begin their day in an elective class at their parent-schools, which begin classes at 7:35 a.m. Students can make their class at the parent-school and still make it back to our campus for the first Alternative class by 9 a.m. The vast majority of our students transported themselves to and from their respective high schools during the school day or utilized the district's bus service to and from their parent- schools at the beginning of and at the end of their school day.

Electives such as Band, Choir, Art, and Vo-tech can be arranged on a half-day schedule, either mornings or afternoons, at the students parent -schools. I explain to parents and students entering the program, that their student's sending school remained their school of record. Their student's diploma would indicate they had graduated from their sending school. "Your son or daughter is still part of their parent-school and may attend or participate in any extracurricular activities sponsored by their parent-school, as long as they meet the standards established by the district governing eligibility." I cautioned our students that once on their parent-school's campus, they were subject to that school's disciplinary policies and should something happen while on campus which resulted in an ISS or OSS assignment, I would not intervene to save them. If they had been suspended from their parent-school, they could not attend classes at the Alternative program either. However, I made it clear to both the student and the parents that the student would be expected in my office at 3 p.m. each day of the suspension or ISS to meet with their teachers, get their assignments, and be on track academically when they returned to the program.

Students enrolled in the Alternative program can request a return transfer to their parent- schools anytime within the first two weeks of an academic semester. Few did so. However, if a student felt in coming to the Alternative program he had misjudged the expectations of the program or just felt the program was not a good fit, he could transfer back into his parent-school. The next student on their school's waiting list would then be notified and scheduled for an enrollment interview. At the end of the two-week transition window, any movement of students into or out of the Alternative program would take place at the beginning of each academic semester.

Many districts assign students to their Alternative programs as the result of disciplinary hearings without providing a way back should things change in the students attitudes and approach to their previous school environment. Effective alternative programs are student-centered and performance-based with regard to their students. Once a student has internalized the behavioral and academic expectations of the program, has experienced academic success on a regular basis, and has expressed a desire to return to his parent school on either a full or part time basis, the district needs a pathway in place for re-integration into the parent-school's environment.

The real test for any Alternative program occurs when a student requests to transfer back to their parent school at the end of the current academic semester. As a principal in an Alternative program, the possibility of a student returning to his parent school is both gratifying and terrifying at the same time. Meeting and talking with the student and his parents about his plans to return to his parent-school at semester is fraught with uncertainties. Can a student who once failed in the previous school setting, return to that setting and succeed? Students entering the program as sophomores or juniors, who feel they have overcome the primary obstacles to their previous success, may choose to return to their parent-schools for their senior year. It's a big step and one that comes from a new sense of empowerment within the individual student. The student has renewed confidence in his/her ability to succeed academically and socially and has internalized the belief that he/she is stronger, more resilient, and ready to succeed.

Conversely, students who, are refusing to attend the program on a regular basis, are unwilling to make an honest academic effort in their classes, are chronically late for school, and are unwilling to accept personal responsibility for their behavior, cannot remain in the program. Without the option of returning non performers to their parent schools at semester, Alternative programs run the very real risk of becoming glorified holding facilities in which students have little or no incentive to change anything about themselves. True Alternative programs are performance- based, both behaviorally and academically. Those students unwilling or unable to meet their commitments must be given every opportunity to do so in an environment supportive of individual change. However, should those changes not occur within a year, the student should be returned to their parent schools with the understanding that they may reapply to the program after one semester.

Counselor Support

An effective and knowledgeable counselor is a godsend to any Alternative principal or teaching staff. Hopefully the counselor will not only be effective with the kids, but also become an important part of the collaborative team. In my experience, the success of an Alternative Education Program, and its longevity, is often the result of a program having a counselor possessing the following attributes:

- Certified by the state in which they employed.

- Knowledgeable of (in state) college or technical program entrance requirements.

- Knowledgeable of financial assistance programs available to graduating students in support of their post secondary educational plans.

- Ability to establish and maintain close working relationships with local colleges and technical programs in order to provide interested students with enrollment contacts, dates of scheduled campus visits, and course catalog information.

- Ability to monitor and maintain individual student transcripts (construct and monitor an Individualized Educational Plan) resulting in the student graduating as scheduled.

- Ability to build relationships with kids and their parents based on open communication, mutual respect, and trust.

- Knowledgeable of specific local service agencies, the services provided by each, and up to date contact information.

- Knowledge of district and local college "dual enrollment" agreements providing graduating seniors the opportunity to earn both high school and college credits while attending an area college on a full time basis.

(All Alternative staff acts as mentors to students enrolled in college classes. Program counselors and teachers alike told our kids that if they ever needed us, either for academic help or simply check in with a familiar face, they were always welcome.)

The program's counselor should attend all student enrollment interviews, and at some point during the interview, review with the student and parents the student's transcript, outlining exactly how many academic credits the student has earned to date and how many credits the student will need to graduate. Together, with the student and the parents, the counselor will build a bridge, semester by semester, moving the student from where he/she is now to where he/she wants to be by a specified time. At the end of the enrollment interview, the student, his parents, and the program's counselor should have an academic plan that if followed by the student will result in he/she graduating from high school.

Work Experience / Community Service

The transition from school to work is an important characteristic of any successful alternative program. Students enrolled in the program's Work Experience classes received one-half credit for having a job and working a minimum of fifteen hours a week. Our program provided a supporting class to assist students in finding and maintaining their jobs, strategies for resolving work place issues, information on emerging employment trends, development of interview skills, resume building, and how to set up and manage individual checking and savings accounts. Students enrolled in the program's On-the-Job classes were supervised by our FACS instructor, who made site visits on a regular basis to discuss her student's performance with their employers then, she would meet with individual students to discuss their employers' feedback and comments regarding their job performance. A well organized, well supervised School-to-Work component provides the program with a positive link to the community at large. Employers experiencing positive results as the result of their hiring an Alternative student will communicate the positives associated with the program to others in the local business community. Such votes of confidence pave the way for future students to find jobs as well as lessen the impact of negative stereotypes within the community and foster a mutually beneficial working partnership between local businesses and the district's Alternative program.

In placing a student with a local business, it is important to emphasize to the student that he shoulders a special responsibility in making sure that the employer who is willing to hire, train, supervise, and pay him, is not given a reason to refuse students in our jobs program employment opportunities in the future. In the same token it is vitally important that students enrolled in the program seek out appropriate employment opportunities. One of Mr. B's special needs students informed him that she had found a job as an exotic dancer in a downtown club. Mr. B came into my office clearly upset. We sat around my big table as he told me that one of student's was employed by a downtown club and not as a server. He had already scheduled a conference with her to inform her that she would not be receiving program support, nor academic credit, as her choice of occupation was not at an approved district site. His quick action probably saved both our jobs and the integrity of the program.

Opportunities for students to engage in Community Service Projects were provided through the Service to School/Service to Community programs. Students could choose from a variety of options ranging from on campus placement to sites located throughout the district or in the community, depending on student interest. Each student received one-half credit for a minimum of sixty hours of service over the course of a semester. Off site placements were restricted to seniors with their own transportation, a valid driver's license, proof of insurance, and their parent's written permission. Each Service to School/Service to Community student was evaluated every Friday by their site supervisor. Their supervisor's written evaluations provided each student with feedback and served as the basis for the student's grade throughout the semester. All student evaluations were kept in an individual student file by the course instructor and were frequently referenced in response to individual student's questions regarding grades or site supervisor comments regarding their performance. Students assigned community service hours by the court could work with our building custodian or instructional staff before or after school to accumulate the required hours. A letter from my office would be sent to their probation officer along with a time sheet, detailing the hours the student had earned in conjunction with the courts order.

School-to-Work programs, in conjunction with a Service-to-School/Service-to-Community component, allow Alternative students to interact with the community at large in a positive manner. Successful Alternative programs work to promote their students in the community, utilize the resources of the community, and provide a framework from which kids become integrated into the mainstream of the communities in which they reside. When Alternative kids connect with their community, everyone wins.

CHAPTER 4

Positive-Based Disciplinary Practices

Be direct, never let anything slide, and always give a kid a way back.

Rules and regulations governing an Alternative Educational environment should be few in number and based on logical consequences. Fewer rules result in the staff and administration focusing on the enforcement of the rules deemed most important. Once specific student behaviors have been identified as "not necessary or inappropriate" the teacher can begin to reinforce students efforts to adjust their behavior. The Big Four constitute the program's non-negotiables with regard to student behavior. They are as follows:

- **No Physical Violence** - (Throw a punch gone before lunch)

- **No Drugs** - (Students must choose between school and substance abuse. The two are not compatible in a public school environment.)

- **No Weapons** - (Students in possession of a weapon will be subject to a district hearing and possible expulsion from the program.)

- **No Verbal Abuse of Staff** - (Respect is a two way street. A teacher must set the standard for student to student, student to teacher, and teacher to student communication in their classrooms. Additionally, teachers must make sure to model their expectations in their day to day verbal interactions with students.)

Violation of any offense listed above may result in a district hearing and possible expulsion from the program.

When a student's behavior violates the "common-sense expectations" of his / her school setting, staff can use the moment to discuss behavioral options with the student, and plan for the future. Not everything can change in a day, but the expectation from staff that change will and should occur (on the part of individual students) is ongoing and should be a part of each conversation between staff and student. Building strong relationships with kids is the key to reducing and in time, extinguishing disruptive student behavior. Daily interactions between instructional staff and their students provide the teacher opportunities to make students aware of which behaviors they need to leave outside the classroom.

Take every opportunity to talk with students informally, in the hallways or lunchroom regarding the plan for surviving class that day. Focus on situations in which he allows his emotions to override his brain and develop a plan to recognize and avoid the "traps" which act as emotional triggers, fueling his negative responses. "Today our job is to stay focused in class and to rise above any perceived provocations." Remind students, "You can't control anyone's behavior other than your own. Just keep your head and let me take care of any situation which arises. If you get caught up in a situation, you are acting as a participant, not as a victim, and will be held accountable for your behavior."

The bottom line is that all students want to be treated fairly in their dealings with authority figures. The individual perceptions of students (and parents) of what constitutes fairness often influences an individual student's response when faced with disciplinary action from a classroom teacher or building principal. In my experience, the worst thing I could do as a classroom teacher or building principal is to treat everyone the same. Students differ emotionally, physically, and mentally, and they respond to teachers based on those differences. A student's perception of fairness is largely based on what happens to other kids who committed the same offense. My response to a student or their parent's claims that I was unfair in dealing with their son or daughter, is to remind them that "they" are different from other students, that the situation which occurred is also very different, and that, although the behavioral expectations for all students remain the same, the pathway for each student to meet those expectations may also be different. Keep in mind not every student sitting in your office requires the same response to a given situation. The goal is to work towards a solution the student can embrace and internalize so we don't have to keep having the same conversation regarding a situation that has already been resolved. In any educational setting, the teachers or principal's approach in speaking with a student regarding inappropriate behavior is the key to diffusing potentially explosive situations. Blind enforcement of the district's disciplinary policies, can result in the creation of a school environment tainted with fear, insecurity and open hostility on the part of both students and their teachers. Listen to the student's version of events. Ask for clarification of the events which occurred and of the student's role in what transpired. Ask for a list of witnesses who may have overheard the conversation or saw what happened. Contact those students and get written statements from each prior to addressing the student seated in your office. Take the time to cover all the bases. Get information from everyone involved.

When interviewing witnesses, it is best to attempt to speak with students who are "non-aligned" with the individuals involved. These students know those involved but have no close ties to any of the participants. Their information regarding the events is usually untainted by an emotional attachment to one individual or another. Kids will lie for their friends, and often do when their emotions take over and a lot of kids are talking about the situation in the hallways. Look for patterns which come from the witnesses statements, and then form conclusions as to what happened prior to contacting the parent. "Based on the statements from students who said they witnessed what occurred, including statements from those students your son named as being able to verify his version of events, here is what I believed happened and why." Lay it all out. Explain to the parent their student's involvement in the incident, and let both the student and the parents know what your response will be and why. For example, a student became upset with his teacher because he refused to begin working on a class assignment. He began arguing with the teacher about the relevance of this assignment. As the discussion escalated, other students in the class chided him to "just shut-up and do his work." One of his friends offered to help him get started and moved to a chair near him. His response was, "Oh hell no!" and he walked out of the classroom. His teacher followed him into the hallway and directed him to go to the office. As he entered my office, I asked him, "Whose class have you left and why?" He sat at my big table and explained to me that he just got angry, but couldn't explain why his emotions had gotten the best of him in Mrs. H.'s class. "So what you're telling me is that you just lost your mind, but now you're better. How many nights this week have you worked until closing? You don't generally have these kinds of issues in class, so I'm wondering if you need to cut back on your hours during the school week and get some more sleep." We talked awhile longer about his job, his success since coming to the program, and of his responsibility to "make things right with Mrs. H."

As a means of providing the student with a way back, we sat at my big table and developed a specific student response plan based on what he needed to do immediately to resolve his issue with the teacher and return to class. I go over each step of the plan with the student and repeat them so there is no confusion or misunderstanding regarding my expectations of the student and the consequences should he fail to meet those expectations. As we walk back to his class, I advise him to knock on his teacher's door and ask if he could speak with her a moment? We practice what he will say when his teacher comes into the hallway; he should apologize to her for his behavior, beg forgiveness, and ask to be readmitted to class with the understanding that this behavior would not happen again. As we approached her door I casually reminded him "If you ever walk out of another teacher's classroom, you should just keep walking." Typically the student will nod his head and knock on the door. I then leave the hallway so that both student and teacher can talk with one another in private and resolve their issues. I return to my office, call the parent to let her know what has transpired and what her son has decided to do to fix the situation he has created. I let her know that he has done the right thing in apologizing to his teacher and returning to class. I told her that she should be receiving a phone call from his teacher regarding the situation today but that I felt everything had been resolved. The underlying message in talking with a kid about his behavior is to state and restate, "Everyone (staff included) is responsible for what he/she says or what he/she does and how it affects those around them."

Teachers and principals will tell you one of their most difficult undertakings is to teach students to shed their victims mentality. Students, for whom behavior has often been an issue, will attempt to justify their inappropriate behavioral responses stating, "If he hadn't said that to me (or about me or hadn't done that to me), I wouldn't have reacted the way I did." They believe that you should be talking with the other student involved and not with them. This response is typical of a student who refuses to accept any personal responsibility for individual behavior and has internalized the belief that once enough injustices have accumulated, he/she is absolved of any responsibility for his/her actions as he is simply defending himself/herself. Holding individual students accountable for their behavior, coupled with staff expectations of behavioral and attitudinal changes on the part of individual students, becomes the basis for student-teacher conflicts. When it becomes clear that a student is unwilling to modify his behavior or accept any responsibility for individual actions, I contact the parents and inform them of our continuing issues with their child regarding behavior in class, and ask for a conference with them, the teacher, the student, and myself. The purpose of the conference is to discuss the situation, and hopefully find a solution. I would ask the parents if the teacher had contacted them regarding the ongoing issues their student is having in the classroom. Often I hear the teacher has contacted the parent repeatedly during the last few weeks, that the parents have talked with their child about the teacher's concerns, and that they "just didn't understand why their child was continuing to have difficulties in the classroom." As any classroom teacher or building principal will tell you, it's is not uncommon for the student's parents to arrive for a conference already upset and ready to paint the teacher as the one most responsible for a long list of problems facing their kid. During the conference stick to the expectation of personal responsibility for individual behavior and always expect the student to meet that standard. Accept no excuses for failure to meet that standard. Work with the student and parents to construct a plan of action to deal with problems should they arise in the future. Before ending the conference make sure that all parties involved understand what is expected from both student and teacher, in resolving the situation, and the consequences if these expectations are not met.

Communication not Confrontation should be the standard for dealing with student misbehavior whether the offense is minor or serious. Enforcement of school rules and regulations should be communicated to the individual student in a low key, honest manner which serves to inform rather than incite the student to further disruptive behaviors. This can be accomplished by taking the student aside and making sure he/she is aware of the specific behaviors that need changing while also providing him/her with "behavioral options" which may lead to his/her being able to solve problems on his/her own. After discussing the situation and possible solutions with a student, I would ask, "What do you think you could do to resolve the situation with Mrs. H and get back on track in her class." I listen as the student explains his/her feelings regarding the situation and what he/she plans to do to fix it. I would then ask, "When are you going to take care of your situation?" stating the situation should be resolved as soon as possible. Helping victim-oriented students build internal controls and assume responsibility for their own behavior is a major first step in reducing the incidence of student initiated disruptions in your building's classrooms and hallways. Once the line had been drawn in the sand regarding what is and is not acceptable student behavior in your program, all instructional staff and administration must enforce the program's disciplinary policies in a fair and consistent manner. Ensure that both parents and students are informed of the program's disciplinary, non-negotiable rules at the enrollment interview. Review the "big four" with your staff, and discuss them with your kids early on so that everyone connected with the program understands what will occur and why when a student violates one of these rules.

Offenses other than the Big Four, such as smoking on campus (anywhere on campus, including the parking lots), student use of the F-word in conversations with peers or staff, or patterns of disruptive classroom behavior (refusing to make an honest effort in class, failure to follow staff directives, leaving class without permission), result in the offending student being assigned restitution by the classroom teacher. If the student refuses to accept the imposition of restitution by the teacher, the student is referred to my office for disposition. Restitution usually entails washing classroom tables, picking up trash on the grounds, washing dishes after lunch, washing tables in the commons after lunch, cleaning cages in the animal lab, etc. All of which are done in conjunction with a phone call to the parents from the teacher. In the call to the parent, the teacher explains the situation and lets the parent know why they offered their student the option of restitution in lieu of ISS or OSS. Restitution options allow the student to stay in class and in school while still being held accountable for his actions. On rare occasions, students will refuse the option of restitution and opt for OSS. When that happens I contact the parents and explain the situation. I tell the parent their child has opted for OSS rather than accept restitution and remain in school for the next three days. In response, the parent will usually ask to speak with their student. Shortly thereafter, the student would hand the phone back to me, and their parent would state their son had decided to accept the restitution assignment and remain in school.

Assignments of restitution in lieu of OSS proved to be an effective means of dealing with minor violations of the program's disciplinary policies. When students began washing tables or putting on a apron to do the lunch dishes, they did so in very public places. Kids sitting around the commons or bringing their trays to the wash area would ask them, "What did you do?" smile, and walk away. Many of them had been in the same situation before and understood what the kid in the apron was experiencing. If a student did a good job, was on time, and cooperative I would tell him, "You did good today. Do the same tomorrow, and we can forget about the third day of your assigned restitution."

One caution regarding the assignment of restitution; it should only be used after you have made the student aware of the inappropriate behavior and have given a verbal warning not to repeat the behavior again while on campus. Restitution assignments made by teachers should be viewed by the administrator as an early disciplinary intervention designed to make the students aware that they need to make immediate changes in behavioral responses in class or while on campus. Assigning restitution as a response to minor violations to the program's disciplinary codes allows teachers and administrators to provide immediate feedback to a student whose behavior is in conflict with the norms of the program without resorting to out-of-school remedies.

A vital component of the Positive Based Disciplinary Practice is communication with the parent on a frequent basis. Instructional staff and administration will find that early and consistent communication with their students parents allows both teachers and principals to avoid parental statements that they never knew their child was having behavioral difficulties or was not in attendance on a regular basis. One parent confided in me that her daughter had missed a total of "167 class periods" before she was notified by the sending school's attendance office. She told the attendance office "that was impossible, as she drove her daughter to school every day and watched as she entered the building before driving away." In talking with her daughter, she discovered that her daughter simply walked in the front door of the building, met her friends, and walked out the back door. Calls home on the part of the classroom teacher to discuss the academic success of their student, to notify parents of school mailings, and to inform them of upcoming exams or assessments will serve you well when you need parental support for any situation which arises involving their son or daughter. The more information a parent has as to the conduct and academic success of their child, the better prepared they are to deal with disciplinary issues when they arise.

To reiterate, always contact the parent in any disciplinary situation. Let them know what has happened, what your plan is regarding their child, listen for any additional options offered by the parent, and let them know that your intention is not to get rid of their kid, but to make your point regarding his or her future behavior. Let the parent know that tomorrow at noon, their child will be washing tables in the commons as a consequence of their behavior. Also, let the parent know that if their child is uncooperative, is late, or does not make an honest effort in completing assigned duties, you will be sending him/her home, pending a parent conference. Ask the parent to talk with their child regarding the situation. Let the parent know that you understand everyone makes mistakes. However, the plan is for kids to learn from their mistakes; and hopefully, not make the same ones again, so they can move on.

Teacher Involvement

You can be a human being and still be an effective classroom teacher.

As an instructor in an Alternative program, you must become a significant other to your students. You must become so important to your students that they are willing to change their behaviors— not because they are frightened of you, but because they have a connection with you.

Staff who become significant others to their students are open, assessable, non-judgmental, and student centered in their interactions with students. They express high expectations for their kids, both behaviorally and academically on a daily basis; and they are unwilling to accept anything less from their students. Students often enter Alternative programs with negative, entrenched, behavior patterns associated with their parent school environments. Their role selections in response to their previous school environment were often those of avoidance, confrontation, and academic failure. In order to alter individual student perceptions regarding their new educational setting, staff, through their relationships with kids, must become catalysts for positive behavioral change. Learn their names, their schedules, be visible, be friendly, talk with them informally about things other than school. In short, staff must be the draw, the reason kids come to school, and the reason kids take the risks necessary to succeed. Kids need positive, honest adult connections.

As a teacher or administrator your refusal to accept anything less from your students, anything other than what is needed for them to succeed, must remain the underlying message, no matter what the conversation. Take every opportunity to encourage them for their willingness to do the little things as well as the big ones which lead to positive change. Remind them that they gave you their word to focus on those behaviors and attitudes which serve as obstacles to their being able to get through a day without disruption. When given the opportunity, always promote options which will lead to individual student personal, social, and academic success. As a significant other to your kids, you'll wear many hats: truant officer, counselor, surrogate parent, teacher, principal, and advocate. Despite what all teachers are taught about becoming too friendly with their students, Alternative teachers/principals know and understand the value of building strong relationships with their kids. Strong, positive student-teacher relationships become the basis for motivating kids to make better choices for themselves. Strong student-teacher relationships help students build the internal controls necessary to rely on their brains rather than their emotions when faced with provocations.

Deal only with the present situation and work towards getting the student to reflect on their Individual Behavior

Should student disciplinary issues arise with staff, the student and the principal should focus only on what occurred that day and what the student needs to do to resolve the situation. Reach an agreement with the student on what needs to be done to make things right. Be specific in terms of how the student should approach the teacher who was wronged or offended by his/her actions. Remind him/her to be aware of his/her body language, focus on what he/she will say, and on the tone of voice. Sincere apologies for inappropriate classroom behavior or disruptions will go a long way in resolving a situation and allowing a student to start fresh in the class the next day. Before the student leaves your office, discuss his/her response should a similar situation occur in the future. Stress to the student that the only behaviors he/she can control are his own, and that the expectation for the future is that you and he/she will not be having this discussion again. Meet with the individual teacher and let him/her know that the student will be coming to see him/her sometime that day to talk about what occurred. Explain to the teacher that the purpose of the conversation is to allow the student to apologize for his/her behavior. As an Alternative principal, you have to strike a balance between support for your teachers and for the efforts of offending students to make things right. Ask the teacher to be receptive and listen to the student's attempts at resolution, even in the face of their very human need to comment on the student's personality or past behavioral issues.

Dwelling on past offenses committed by a student communicates unwillingness on the part of the teacher to truly resolve the immediate issue. Giving lip service in response to a student's attempts to apologize for classroom behavior only serves to detract from the teacher's ability to deal effectively with the student in the future and provides the student with an out: "I tried to tell her that I was sorry for my behavior in her class today, but she wasn't interested in anything I was trying to say." Education is an investment in human potential. Students need opportunities to practice and internalize appropriate responses in dealing with authority figures. Apologizing for inappropriate behavior is one way a student can practice the skills necessary to resolve situations without resorting to emotional confrontations. In discussing with a student, the behaviors which violate the program's expectations, make sure you take the time to ensure that the student understands why their behavior is unnecessary and counterproductive. Express your comments in a low key and non-threatening manner, compromise when you can, and provide the offending student a framework in which he/she can begin to change the negative behavior. "This is a good place for you. You're doing well here. Why waste your time and energy getting caught up in this nonsense? Today you made poor choices in response to your situation, tomorrow we start fresh, but when you walk through those doors in the morning, it's with the understanding that today will be different than yesterday."

As a principal, once you've drawn a line in the sand regarding your expectations of an individual student's behavior, make it a priority to follow up with the student prior to dismissal for the day. I waited for L by the front door or in the parking lot and would casually ask her if she had taken care of business? If L's answer was "yes", I thanked her for doing so, and told her I'd see her tomorrow. Then, I'd go talk with the teacher to make certain that L complied with my request and spoken with her teacher and resolved the situation. It's important at this point to discuss with the teacher what happened that day, and ask about the plan for tomorrow when L walks into the room. Discuss what they'll do in response to a similar situation should it occur again. I suggested the teacher wait outside the door as the student approaches the classroom, take her aside and tell L we can't have a day in class today like the one we had yesterday. I simply suggested to the teacher to give L two redirections if her behavior becomes disruptive, and should the teacher have to redirect L a third time, ask her to leave the class and complete her work at the table in the hallway. Also, let the teacher know if it becomes necessary for L to leave the classroom, L is to be told that she will not be welcome back until both you and the principal have scheduled a conference with her parents.

As a principal I can't stress enough the importance of discussing and reviewing with the teacher the expectations for the student prior to her walking into the class the next day. At some point during the next school day (preferably before the student is scheduled to attend class) the teacher needs to quietly and casually communicate the expectations for her in class that day. As building principal I would also seek out L and remind her of the plan to both survive and succeed academically, of her role in making today better than yesterday, and most importantly remind L "If you can't stay in class, you can't stay in the program." If things go well; thank the student for their efforts. Contact their parents to let them know that today their child handled the class well, and hopefully, learned from her mistakes, and is ready to move on.

It's making the effort to ensure that all parties have met their obligations regarding a specific situation that makes the difference in diffusing future disciplinary issues before they escalate into disruptive classroom incidents. The difference for students will be in the experience of being held accountable for their behavior on a daily basis. The difference for the program will be fewer disciplinary issues in the classroom resulting from power struggles with students whose behavioral issues continue to dominate their interactions with staff.

If, on the other hand, in asking the student at the end of the day if she took care of business, and the answer is "no", I asked her why she didn't keep her word? I let the student know that tomorrow morning would be a good time to go find her teacher and to set things right. I follow up our conversation with another call to L's parents letting them know what happened and why I feel it's necessary for L to talk with her teacher and resolve the situation before attending the class again. I communicate my expectations that L will comply with my request that she speak with the teacher when she arrives on campus the next day. I ask for their assistance in reinforcing L's plan of action for resolving her issues in her classroom. State to the parent the end goal is for all issues to be resolved so that L can begin to move on in the class. As I walk the parking lot the next morning, I watch for L driving onto the lot, and then, I move towards her car so that when she emerges from her car I am there to say "Good morning." As we walk towards the front doors I let L know the teacher is in the classroom now, and I walk L to the classroom door. Along the way we discuss what L's going to say and how she's going to say it. I wait outside of the classroom for her to come out and ask her how things went. I ask if she is going to survive the class today. I let L know that I "have absolute faith in her being able to handle herself in class today." And, I also explain to L, "If anyone says anything to him or behaves towards him in a way he feels is threatening or provocative, she is to let the teacher know immediately." I remind L to let the teacher do their jobs. "Your job is to focus, work, and not get caught up in any nonsense which may occur." I remind L that the only behavior she can control is her own. If a situation occurs, she is expected to "be bigger than the situation, let it slide, and get on with the business of getting a high school diploma."

Work towards getting the student to make a plan to change inappropriate behavior and hold them to it.

*What are we going to do next time you begin
to feel yourself becoming angry?*

It's a fine line between advocating for a student and respecting the need for classroom teachers to do their job. Constant disruptions and negative displays of strong emotions run counter to the day to day insistence of the principal that staff work to help problem students find a more appropriate way to express themselves in class. On many occasions after a long day, while listening to the struggles of staff with a particular student, I remind them that they don't realize how good they are at what they do. I also remind them, "If it were easy, anyone could do it."

The best laid plans often prove less than effective when a student repeatedly disrupts class and teachers find themselves out of options. When a student is repeatedly sent to the office for disruptive classroom behavior, the student and the teacher have clearly reached a point where neither is capable of resolving the situation. Then it's time to sit down with the student, the teacher, and the parents to discuss options for the student in the class. Prior to the meeting, both the teacher and the student need to write down the three most pressing issues each feels needs to be resolved in order for each to be successful in the classroom. Consequences for failing to meet the agreed on expectations can't really be discussed until both student and teacher have had their say. Once that has happened, the focus of the discussion should be on recognition, cooperation and compliance.

After each has spoken, the principal should paraphrase what both the teacher and student have said and propose a possible solution to resolve the negative situation. The message conveyed by the principal is that both the student and the teacher are accountable for implementing a solution so both can get back to doing their respective jobs in the class.

Each participant should be given a copy of the written contract which was signed by the teacher, student, parents, and administrator summarizing the discussion and specifically listing the consequences for failing to meet the tenets of the agreed on contract. For example, if after two redirects by the teacher, the student has not complied with the teacher's requests, the student will be asked to leave class, go to Mr. Gann's big office table, and complete their assignment. The teacher will contact the student's parents and notify them of what occurred that day in class. The administrator will also contact the student's parents and notify them that their child will be kept out of Mr. L's class for the next two school days until the administrator can investigate what occurred in Mr. L's class as well as give both Mr. L and W some breathing space. I informed the parents that W would have the assignments from Mr. L's class and that he can work on his assignments at my big table during his Block Five class. The next morning I went to Mr. L's classroom to get W's assignments. The student had become angry and had walked out of the class, but I (as the administrator) needed some clarification as to why. After discussing the incident with Mr. L he got W's assignments and waited for him at the front door. As we walked to my office I explained to him, that in his being asked to leave Mr. L's classroom, he had violated his agreement and for the remainder of the week (two days), and he would be completing his Block Five assignments at my big table. I asked him "What happened?" and listened to his explanation. I related to him Mr. L's version of events explaining to him why Mr. L thought it necessary for him to remain out of his class for the next two days, but I expected him to return to Mr. L's class on Monday. W denied the teacher's version of events and stated that, "I have no idea why I was kicked out of class." W bluntly said "I hate Mr. L and want out of his class." I reminded W that he had given me his word to work towards finding a solution to his issues in Mr. L's class and I expected him to keep it. "It doesn't matter if you hate him or not. You need the credit to graduate. You have X number of days until you graduate, just suck it up, nod your head in the appropriate places, and don't give him a reason to be involved with you in a negative way." I contacted W's parents and related, to the best of my knowledge, what had happened. I told his parents that I had listened to his side of the story and had spoken with other students in the class who, he indicated, would support his version of events. In my conversations with the witnesses, it was evident that they were unsure of what happened. They knew that W. had become upset and had walked out of Mr. L's classroom. I explained to W's parents that W was expected to overcome whatever issues he had with Mr. L. and return to class on Monday ready to take care of business. W's parents and I discussed my suggestion to keep W out of Mr. L's class tomorrow and use the time to discuss, with W, a plan for him to return to Mr. L's class on Monday. I listened W's parents discussed their concerns about the personality conflict which they felt existed between W and Mr. L. I responded that W needed the credit to graduate, that Mr. L was the only instructor for the course, and that her son needed to "just suck it up and survive for a few more days until he graduated." After talking with W's parent, I went to Mr. L's classroom to notify him that W. would be returning to his classroom on Monday. I reminded Mr. L that he needed to ensure that W was given every opportunity to succeed in his class, but to stick to the agreement reached in conference with his parents. I also informed Mr. L that W's parents had been contacted and it was made plain to them that W was responsible for his behavior in class and that he was expected to return to class on Monday without further incident. In talking with Mr. L I wanted to assure him that I supported him in his attempts to maintain discipline in his class, but I also wanted to stress that he give W every opportunity to succeed in his class. In the course of our discussion it was suggested that Mr. L keep a daily log summarizing any interactions he had with W regarding academics, behavior, and general conversations. Before leaving Mr. L's classroom I once again stressed that he make the supreme effort to ensure that W was given no justification for any negative comments that he might make to his parents regarding Mr. L's approach towards him in class. Mr. L was also cautioned that W's parents were concerned about a personality conflict which they felt he had with their son and would jump at the chance to paint him as acting in an unfair manner towards their son should another issue arise.

Having the specifics regarding a situation from both the teacher's and the student's perspective enables me as an administrator to address the concerns of all parties in an informed manner. Every informal conversation with the student in the hallway, commons area, or parking lot is an opportunity for the principal to support the student's efforts to succeed in the class. "You made the week. You're doing a good job in the class. You'll be walking across the stage in a matter of a few days. Just do your job and graduate."

As an Alternative principal I encouraged my staff to meet daily to discuss students concerns. During these times, we worked together in support of one another. When all the staff is aware of a situation, each one has the opportunity to reinforce the message to the student in hallways, at lunch, and in the student seating area. Casual interactions with students throughout the school day are a hallmark of Alternative educational programs. For example, I would man the serving line on Friday's asking students what they wanted on their sandwiches. In that short time, between asking if a student wanted pickles or peppers, I could address specific issues with specific students. I could ask them if they had taken care of business in a specific classroom or what they intended to do about finding a job as they needed a work study credit to graduate. There are no secrets in an alternative program. Every student quickly learns that the staff talks with one another every day before and after school. Every teacher knows what's happened, who was involved, and the plan to fix the situation. Staff expectations for student behavior and academic performance are shared and verbalized with students in a quiet, direct, and caring manner. Students quickly realize there is no escape. Teachers understand they must "hang together or they will surely hang separately."

The program's commitment to Positive Based Disciplinary Practices is reinforced by the belief in the educational equivalent of the old saying, "Give a man a fish he can eat for a day; Teach him how to fish, he can eat for a lifetime." Based on that philosophy, our staff began from day one to inform a student rather than confront a student whose behavior or words were disruptive and unnecessary. Taking the time to teach students how to manage their own individual behavior, is preferable to the staff having to waste valuable instructional time dealing with student misconduct on a daily basis. The chart below contrasts the philosophies of Positive- Based Disciplinary Practices utilized by true Alternative programs with those often practiced by traditional school administrators and teachers.

Behaving Responsibly Is More Valued Than Behaving Obediently

ALTERNATIVE ENVIRONMENT	TRADITIONAL ENVIRONMENT
Relationship Oriented: Personal responsibility for individual behavior.	Power Oriented: No personal responsibility for individual behavior.
Internal Controls: Initiated by Student	External Controls: Done to student
Options in Response to Student Misbehavior: Student choices	Limited Options to Student Misbehavior: Policy and Procedures
Individual Ownership of Behavior: Avoid victims mentality	No Individual Ownership of Behavior: Don't get caught; blame others
Individual Responsibility for Behavior: Absence of "scapegoating". Opportunities for real change to occur.	External Authority Responsible for Individual: Attitude of "You have to catch me; then prove I did it."

The keys to Positive Based Discipline Practices begin with changing the individual perceptions of students regarding their school environments. Many of our students stated that they felt no connection to their previous schools, that they felt they just didn't fit in and were not accepted for who they were. In true Alternative programs, the reliance on strong, positive relationships between staff and students creates a foundation for real change in student's perception of where he fits in his school setting. Student-teacher relationships based on mutual trust, honesty, and high expectations for student success, both academically and behaviorally, allow the individual student to experiment with different behavioral responses to situations which previously resulted in an explosion of negative behaviors, prompting negative responses from the instructional staff and building administration as well. Opportunities for students to explore different ways of dealing with situations in which their strong emotions overtake their rational thought process is possible when interacting with a caring and supportive adult. Students, experiencing chronic discipline issues in which they refuse to accept any personal responsibility for their behaviors, are doomed to repeat both the behaviors, and to mentally and emotionally reinforce their belief that they are victims of an unfair and repressive system which exists to deny them an effective voice. Strong relationships between staff and students provide a framework for changing the students perspective of their school environment and allows students more flexibility in determining their choice of roles in response to their interactions with instructional staff and peer group.

The emphasis on student acceptance of personal responsibility for individual behavior, for controlling strong emotions in the face of perceived provocations, and for seeking solutions, rather than confrontation, is possible when students are made aware of different behavioral options in response to a situation. The power to choose from a variety of options coupled with the encouragement and support from the instructional staff for a student to explore and adopt new ways of responding to situations is a major component of a student learning to reflect on their behavior rather than seek an emotional confrontation when in conflict with an authority figure. The process for a student to begin building internal controls is an investment in changing entrenched negative behavioral responses and replacing them with positive based responses. This will not be accomplished through the imposed position of get tough policies on the part of administrators, or in an attempt by a classroom teacher to instill fear in their students as a classroom management tool. While serving as an Assistant Principal in a traditional junior high, a veteran teacher commented to me that they, being students," are not scared of you." I responded that the office can never "punish a kid enough to get them to change their behavior." Rather than change, it's easier for a kid to just avoid or ignore any attempts by someone to get them involved in finding solutions to their own school related issues. Although the teacher and I had many conversations dealing with his classroom management issues, he was unable to make the leap from a punitively oriented classroom to a relationship oriented classroom and retired at semester. In coming to my office to inform me he was retiring, he indicated that he felt he could no longer deal effectively with the emerging behavioral issues associated with teaching in an urban classroom. He felt it was just no longer worth the aggravation and needed to leave. I wished him well.

The patience to self-reflect, to review options, to anticipate consequences, and to change behavioral responses comes about as the result of an individual student feeling a connection with a teacher or administrator who is willing to invest in the potential of a kid. Helping a student accept that he is solely responsible for his behavior, and to reject his role of victim, is often a long road for both the student and staff. Be consistent, be fair, and hold each student accountable for their individual behavior. Preach alternatives, and options in response to an individual student's inappropriate behavior. Remind students that they are not a victim if they had a role in what occurred and as a result of their behavior, they share in the responsibility for finding a solution to the situation. Providing alternatives on a daily basis to entrenched behaviors is both time consuming and necessary. When things go south for a kid and he has been sent out of class for displays of strong negative emotions, I ask him; "What did your behavior accomplish? Did it resolve the situation? What could you have done differently to reduce your level of frustration? What's your plan for next time?" When calm has been restored and the student is beginning to think instead of just reacting, he is able to agree on a plan for dealing with the situation. I expect my staff to create the expectations for future behavior and communicate those expectations to individual students rather than issue ultimatums. I also expect my staff to contact the parents to let them know what is going on, what the plan is, and enlist their support for trying a new approach to an old problem. I expect no less from myself when dealing with students violations of the program's norms. And when kids complain about other students who go out of their way to annoy them, I ask, "Who is in charge of you? Why do you give them so much power over you? All they have to do is say this or do that and you're off to the races emotionally." Kids often respond, "It's not my fault. If they hadn't said that to me or done that to me, I wouldn't have had to react the way I did." However, I never deviate from the message that they are the only one who controls their own behavior.

Students who refuse to accept personal responsibility for their individual behavior are playing the ultimate victim's game. They are often angry, upset, and attempt to use their frequent displays of strong emotion as policing mechanism designed to manipulate and control the behaviors of those around them. They pose major problems for any staff committed to the premise of Positive Based Disciplinary Practices and are often supported in their commitment to victimhood by their parents, who reinforce their reliance on scapegoating as a tool to justify and excuse their child's behavior. I often refer to their situation as the "Clint Eastwood Syndrome." If you've ever watched the spaghetti westerns produced in the late 1960's featuring Mr. Eastwood, whose character spends much of the film seeking retribution for wrongs done to him by the films bad guys, revels in his victims mentality over the course of the film, as the blood flies and the body count mounts as he, and by extension the audience, exacts justice. At-risk kids many times reflect the same mentality when dealing with their inability to control their emotional responses to perceived provocations on the part of their peers or authority figures. Once they have collected enough injustices, they are free to respond as they feel regardless of how inappropriate their behavior is in relation to the perceived provocation. As long as they believe someone else is ultimately responsible for what they do and what they say, they feel justified in their reactions, and absolve themselves of any personal responsibility for their behavior. It's a tough situation and one that is not easily remedied by staff. I advise staff to stay on message with both student and parents and continue to hold students accountable for their individual behavior in the face of the student and his parents intransigence. As the staff and I would talk at the end of the day, they would lament their efforts to get an individual student to stop scapegoating and accept responsibility for his/her own behavior. I would listen and encourage them not to give up. After all tomorrow is another day.

A good rule of thumb for any Alternative teacher or principal reflecting on the day is a simple one: When you begin to doubt your effectiveness in dealing with a particularly difficult student or parent or situation, look at yourself in the mirror and ask yourself this question, "Did I do everything I could today to make a positive difference in a kid life?" If the answer to that question is "yes," you've had a good day at school. If the answer to that question is "no," then you'd better go back to school tomorrow with a plan to fix the situation. As long as you're committed to returning the next day to fix any situation you feel you didn't handle well, there is hope for all of your students to succeed.

Notes on Reflection

As a principal in an Alternative program, I must be visible and accessible to students throughout the day. My classroom/office served as a place where kids could come in for a few moments and touch base (I never spent that much time in my office during the day anyway). Picking through the bowl of Jolly Ranchers, to find their favorite flavor, served as their motivation to initiate a conversation. Kids loved them, and they helped the nicotine addicts get through the school day. Kids came in to get candy and listen to the music I was playing on my ghetto blaster. It was usually a casual conversation, but necessary, if you were a kid struggling with your emotional responses on a daily basis. Just touching base, getting some encouragement, some acknowledgement of their ongoing struggle, seemed to help them get through another class period without incident.

Classroom teachers need to remember that obedience for obedience sake is a poor classroom management plan. The "do it or else mentality" is bad for both teachers and students. The same battles, with the same kids, will be fought day after day. It will increase tension levels in the classroom; teachers will smile less, and begin to verbalize to their colleagues how they dread thinking about their fifth period class. In discussions about kids in the lounge, teachers will find themselves immersed in the "If I could just get rid of so and so, my class would be manageable" mentality. Sometimes that's true; however, once that student is gone from the class, there'll be another one to take his/her place. Classroom teachers, who rely on the institutionalized power of their positions to maintain classroom discipline, often find themselves locked in daily struggles with their students, who are masters at playing the "you have to catch me game" or the "you're not the boss of me game." Also, if you don't catch me, it is ok for me to do it." Everything depends on who has the greater power on any given day. Kids realize they have the power to disrupt; they know which buttons to push to get a teacher rolling, even in the face of certain punishment, and nothing ever gets resolved. It's a no-win situation for everyone.

Just as a man who can fish will never starve students who accept responsibly for their own behavior will become an asset to the program. Once students begin to feel comfortable in their new skin, their perspective changes regarding their school and the roles they select. Students, once labeled as chronic disciplinary problems, evolve into leaders, mentors, and graduates. Students, who see themselves as successful, as being part of an environment in which the people they care about also care about them, become strong advocates for the program with their peers, their parents, and the community. (They also become eligible for the "Shit Head to Scholar Award" which is awarded to the student demonstrating the greatest positive change in any given year or semester as voted by the staff). As I sat in the student seating area talking with soon to be graduating seniors, our conversations invariably turned to how much they had changed since entering the program. I reminded them of situations they often found themselves in as first-year students and of how many times I had to discuss their behavior with them in my office. We laughed as I told J that I liked the new J a lot more than the old J; and as the result of his turning himself around, I was nominating him for this year's "Shit Head To Scholar Award." J just grinned and thanked me. I mentioned my conversation with J to the staff, and they agreed that he had made tremendous progress. He had become a real human being. Later that day as I walked down our hallway, I saw J in conversation with another student outside the boys bathroom. His posture and mannerisms indicated he was up to something other than simply going to the bathroom. As I approached him, he turned and made eye contact with me. As I walked past him I said "remember you're a nominee." He smiled, ducked his head, and moved towards class. A simple statement from an individual with whom J had a relationship was enough to head off any inclination of misbehavior on his part.

As a principal and teacher, I made it a priority to (gather kids in my classroom/office) to discuss a situation which had occurred, or one I felt was about to occur, and ask for their help in making sure that things stayed on an even keel. Even on days when veteran students reverted to their "old ways" in response to something that happened, they recovered more quickly and recognized what they must do to resolve the situation and get themselves back on track. In short, they had internalized the behavioral norms of their environment and in doing so, strengthened their bond with the staff, the program, and most importantly, viewed themselves as capable of, and deserving of, success.

Individual choice is a powerful motivator for change, and the expectation that a student will begin to utilize choice with regard to his/her behavior is a true first step towards reducing peer conflicts and negative contacts with authority figures both in the community as well as in school. Individual choice also improves students self-image, and provides a foundation for students to view themselves and their situations through the eyes of an individual no longer a slave to their emotions.

CHAPTER 5

Alternative Education Programs in Support Of Traditional Schools

Alternative Education Programs create opportunities for a school district to reach a specific student population which has effectively disengaged itself from the district's educational mainstream. By offering estranged, secondary students alternatives to the traditional school setting, districts are signaling to their communities that they see value in providing "lost kids" a pathway to reconnect with their schools and community. True Alternative programs that offer students a second chance to graduate are not meant as terminal programs. Their purpose is to provide an educational environment in which students can develop and internalize the academic and behavioral skills necessary for them to return to their parent school environment and succeed. The district's implementation of a true Alternative Education Program in support of its traditional educational programs may result in at-risk kids having opportunities to experience:

Increased Attendance and Commitment

Student's perceptions of their educational environment as "different" from that of the traditional school in which they were academically, socially, unsuccessful is a major foundation of any successful Alternative Education Program. When at-risk kids are asked to explain the differences between their program and the traditional setting, they often comment on their interactions with an instructional staff, who they describe as committed to their individual success and skilled at relationship building. Having a relationship with a caring adult at school, coupled with the student's immersion into an educational environment characterized by support and structure results in his/her feeling a part of something special. Students feelings of acceptance are reinforced daily through their interactions with staff that will support their efforts to succeed while communicating the programs expectations of regular school attendance, honest academic effort, and acceptance of personal responsibility for individual behavior. An individual student's connection to his/her school increases dramatically when the adults he/she cares about, are committed to the shared goals of personal, social, and academic success for all students.

Increased Self-confidence, Responsibility, and Ownership

An individual student's choice to enter or leave an Alternative Education Program is crucial to establishing and maintaining an individual student's commitment to the program and his/her role in it. Students who choose to become part of an Alternative program are more likely to act in support of the program's expectations than those students assigned to the district's Alternative program by their districts hearing officer or building administrators as a result of chronic academic failure, absenteeism, or disciplinary issues. Personal ownership of a program, a sense of belonging and acceptance as a member of a supportive community provides students with the motivation to achieve, succeed, and graduate. Once students have experienced school related success, they begin to see themselves as having personal value, and the program itself as something which they have a vested interest in protecting and promoting.

Opportunities for Instructional Staff to Design And Implement Innovative Instructional Programs Based On The Needs Of Individual Students.

I advised staff every semester to "get to know your kids as quickly as possible." Learn their names, talk with them about their previous school environments and about why they did or did not succeed in their parent schools. Many of my students told me that they had always made the Honor Roll until they entered Middle School; then, things began to change for them with regard to their willingness to take their school environments seriously. They began to feel disconnected from their school, from their grades, and they no longer participated in school activities. School seemed less important and became more trouble than it was worth. Many future Alternative kids dropped out (in place) during their middle school years.

Once the academic information regarding your child's individual learning styles, reading and math levels, is made available, a teacher can begin to build a curriculum for each student based on his/her strengths. Not every student has to work from the same materials in class, nor does every student have to move at the same pace. If you have kids "who get it" and need to move on, provide a framework for them to do so. Individualize the curriculum to address the ability levels of students, utilize peer helpers in class, and contact members of community organizations which may be willing to become mentors in math and reading classes. Provide kids a variety of pathways with which they can utilize to explore or experiment as they work towards completing their assigned work. For example, in studying a lesson on cells, students may choose from a variety of assignment presentation options whether that be artistic in nature, drawing a 3-D representation of specific cells in various stages of development, or using creative cartooning to depict the birth of a cell, or by chronicling the life of a cell in prose, a poem or a short story. Writing and performing a rap song identifying the components of a cell, (sing the song, recall the information), or writing and directing students in a one act play depicting the drama of a cell in its final death throes are effective assignment presentations. Alternative teachers are encouraged to promote educational options; including traditional paper and pencil exams. Students succeed in Alternative programs because they have a relationship with their teachers, who are not tied to traditional methods of instruction, and who allow their kids the freedom to express their knowledge based on their individual academic strengths.

As an Alternative classroom teacher you can be DIFFERENT in your approach to implementing the district's curriculum, you can be EFFECTIVE as a change agent for your kids, and become a **significant**

other in their lives. Focus efforts on designing academic lessons which reinforce kids strengths while continuing to improve their efforts in the specific (academic) areas they may still find difficult to master. Building partnerships with students and helping them to gain confidence in their ability to succeed is far more important than adhering to the "common assessment, common curricular approach" utilized by districts more concerned with maximizing district test scores than meeting the individual needs of their kids.

Alternative programs provide a structure for developing "parallel district" curriculums in support of individual students. The end goal remains the same, one in which students can prove mastery of a specific subject to the extent that they can legitimately receive academic credit for their efforts. However the pathway towards that mastery may involve a variety of instructional approaches specifically geared towards a student's individual learning style, interests, and ability level. Educational approaches, which encourage and enhance individual student strengths while working to recognize and improve areas of academic weakness, provide a student with "options" in support of academic success rather than the "one shoe fits all" approach found in many traditional classrooms. The flexibility of Alternative classrooms allows every teacher to construct curricular approaches which are tailored to the needs of individual students. As an Alternative administrator and classroom teacher, I would often counsel young staff members not to worry about the demands of the educational bureaucracy or about how few chapters they've covered in the approved text or about impending state assessments. I advised them to focus their efforts on building an environment in their classroom that works for their kids, and not to worry so much about the educational "who-ha's" who tout the quality of their district's educational programs in terms of district and state assessments scores.

Increased Positive Interactions between Parents, Students, and Instructional Staff

Everyone enjoys success. Parents want their children to succeed and be recognized for their successes. Parental support for Alternative programs increases as their child's feelings of personal success and academic achievement levels rise. When a parent feels that their student is understood, treated fairly, and held accountable for academic effort or the lack of it, they promote the program as worthwhile and effective. Many parents entering their initial interview with the program's counselor or principal express fears that their son or daughter would ever graduate from high school, or if they did, will graduate with a grade point average so unimpressive that they would have to settle for a state school in the unlikely event that their student would be accepted to any institution other than a community college. Once students began to experience school related success and build connections to their school, parents would express their surprise that their child "now got herself/himself up in the mornings and wanted to come to school." They were happy that the daily battles surrounding attendance had ended and with the new attitude that their child exhibited towards school and to making her/his grades.

The Academy was a word of mouth program. Parents talked about the program and its positive impact on their kids both at home and with other parents in the grocery store or over a connecting back fence. In conversations with the parents of prospective students, they often commented on their discussions with the parents of current students as a reason for their interest in the program. Committed, successful students result in committed, involved parents, who in turn support the program's instructional staff, administration, and school mission, resulting in a win-win environment for all involved.

Decreased Instances of School Related Violence, Vandalism, Expulsions, and Dropouts.

Students who experience school related success, who feel a part of their school, and who feel a connection to their teachers, are less likely to engage in negative behaviors involving their school. They are also more likely to protect and defend their school environment against those students who seek to disrupt or damage the program in any way. In my experience, incidents of vandalism directed against the Alternative program, were rare and often met with student commitments to take care of the situation themselves. Student violence directed against staff was non- existent. The relationships between staff and students were often so strong that a student would intervene on behalf of a classroom teacher experiencing compliance issues with a student. It was not uncommon for a veteran student to lean over from his desk and tell a disruptive student, "He told you to turn to page 56. Do it and shut the fuck up!" In response I would ask to see my defender after class and remind him that I was capable of taking care of disciplinary issues in my class. I would thank him for his support but suggest that he find a different way to express his feelings in class. I would also speak with the student, whose behavior and lack of focus disrupted my class, and advise him in the future to save his posturing for the community, not my classroom. Kids who feel secure, safe, and successful are very conscious of those students, who in their words "Don't belong here, Who are here for the wrong reasons or Who don't care about the program." Veteran students are not shy about "calling an individual student out" in defense of a teacher or the program in general, and they play an important role in socializing new students to the norms of the program.

Expulsions from the program were infrequent and imposed only for the most serious violations of the program's and district's policies. Recommending the removal of a student from the program was always a difficult and gut wrenching decision. Even if deserved by a student, I believe there are absolutes regarding individual student behavior; and when those lines have been crossed by a student, a student's removal from the program is justified and necessary to maintain the integrity of the program.

Over the eleven years I served as principal and teacher at the Blue Valley Academy, we averaged a graduation rate of (91%) compared with a drop-out rate of less than (5%) over the same time frame. Kids, deciding to leave the program, came into my office to notify me of their decision and to discuss "their other" options as well as to tell me their reasons for leaving the program. The vast majority of kids needed to deal with a personal issue or needed to work full time to support their cars and apartments, or needed to deal with a family issue spiraling out of control. In talking with them about their decision, they would invariably talk about their connection to the program and its teachers. After listening to them I would ask, "Now explain to me again why you're leaving the program?" What students really wanted from me was not my approval or support for their decision; but assurance that when their stint in rehab, or jail, or when they found a place to live, or if they didn't do well in pursuit of a GED or other educational options, they could return to the program. I would listen to their explanations and then remind them that they would always be Academy kids, and always welcome here if things did or did not work out for them.

Opportunities For The Traditional School To Review/Evaluate Current Practices and Policies Relating To Individual Student Success

Which factors lead to academic, personal, and social success for a student in one educational environment and dismal failure in another? Traditional teachers will tell you that those same students, who once failed their core classes and are now experiencing academic success in an Alternative environment, are doing so because the Alternative programs standards for measuring its students' academic success are much lower than those of the traditional schools. The question, most frequently asked by traditional teachers of Alternative staff, centers around their feeling that Alternative kids are being spoon fed academics and lauded for their successes; "Are students enrolled in a Biology class doing the same level of work as those students enrolled in the same course in a traditional school?" The answer is both "Yes and No." Yes, Alternative students are exposed to the same information from the same texts used by traditional school teachers, but the approach taken by the Alternative teacher in working with individual students may be completely different. Are Alternative teachers covering the same amount of content as teachers in a traditional class? "No" but the content they do cover is taught in such a way that all students can demonstrate their mastery of the information presented based on the individual students primary learning style.

Emulating the teacher-student relationships, found in virtually all successful Alternative programs, is rejected by the majority of traditional school teachers and administrators for a variety of reasons. First and foremost is the increasing size of large urban and suburban schools whose enrollment often exceeds well over a thousand students in many instances. The lack of time, the demands of district office (they love committees and meetings), dwindling resources, the commitment of class time to ensure that students are prepared for state and district assessments, expanding class sizes, (my daughter will begin this school year with (38) first and second graders and no aide), and the list goes on.

Public school environments should exist to promote the well being of their students as their first priority. **The individual success or failure of a student should never be viewed as a by-product of an educational system.** The traditional schools focus on maintaining the system, even in the face of growing student estrangement, is at best short sighted and at worst criminal, resulting in a dropout rate of 25% or higher for some minority groups. The system itself is never seriously examined to ensure that its focus is student-centered rather than content centered. The theory being that it's not the system that failed the student but the student who failed himself. As teachers we can do better.

(Note to author: Climb down off your soapbox and get back to the topic at hand.)

Opportunities do exist for traditional schools to integrate successful alternative behavioral and academic practices into their approach to kids, but they are often squandered by the unwillingness of teachers and administrators in both programs to put aside their prejudices and work together for the common good of all kids. Alternative Education Programs provide district staff with options for teachers tired of maintaining the status quo and who have "the calling" to teach in a different way, in a totally different educational environment. Only a district's best and most dynamic teachers should be considered for teaching positions in an Alternative program. Their creativity, drive, knowledge, and tenacity, coupled with their belief that they can (and will) make a positive difference in a kid life, constitutes the lifeblood of a successful Alternative program.

Whether you're teaching in a traditional school or in an Alternative program remember that our profession represents the only social institution committed to providing an environment in which kids are free to explore, experiment, discover, and embrace their potential for success. It's a big job; but if we do it right, if we always act in the best interest of kids, we, as teachers, can be assured of the answer when we look ourselves in the mirror each evening and ask, "Did I do everything I could to make a positive difference in a kid's life today?"

CHAPTER 6

Program Longevity: The Art of Survival

In my twenty-five years as an Alternative program principal, I found one of the toughest and most time consuming aspects of my job was not dealing with my kids or their families but dealing with the demands and expectations of district office officials. Our priorities were often in conflict, as were our philosophies regarding how to manage instructional staff, adherence to district policies, and the general consensus among district administrators that teachers comprised the largest stumbling block to implementing district office initiatives. When I felt overwhelmed, after having left a three hour meeting in which I had been instructed to prepare a lengthy report detailing how I planned to implement the latest district office initiative in my building, I would panic and then realize that "it's only rock-n-roll." As the Alternative program principal, I could get away with "tweaking the noses" of specific district office personnel on occasion. After all I was expected to be a little different than the rest of the district's administrative staff; but to blatantly ignore the politics associated with being an administrator in any district can have negative consequences. Although tempting, it's never a good idea to openly confront authority. When you do, you only strengthen it. Throughout my career as an Alternative principal and teacher, I found that the best way to deal with authority figures, especially those you have no use for, is through circumvention, humor, and ridicule; good counter-culture training.

Remember, if you're going to be different, you had better be very good at your job. It also helps to have an advocate at district office that has the unqualified support of the Board. Alternative program principals need someone with whom they can build a relationship, who understands their program, has insight into how they think, and who will run interference for them when their detractors come to them with complaints about them and their reluctance to "get on board" in support of the latest educational wave sweeping the nation and the district. The program's advocate serves as liaison to the Board, other district office officials, and the sending school principals.

Invite your supervisor and board members to the program's opening day festivities. Encourage them to stand with you at the front door to welcome students and parents to the first day of school. Providing a pancake breakfast for our kids, their parents, and inviting district officials to attend is a long standing tradition on the first day of school and is a positive way to begin a new school year. As a principal I needed to reinforce the relationships begun with my kids and their parents during our initial interview. Standing in front of my building and welcoming kids by their first names proved to be a major building block with parents, who would comment to their kids as they walked past me, "He already knows your name." It also provided me with an opportunity to reconnect with board members and to have them experience first-hand the positive impact of their decision to implement the program.

The first two weeks of a program were viewed by the staff and me as the "honeymoon phase." Kids are getting acclimated to the norms of the program, their classes, and their teachers. As the year progresses and kids begin to exhibit their true selves in terms of their personalities, behavioral responses to staff, and issues which arise in the community, teachers need the involvement, the counsel, and the direction of their supervisor in weathering the storms associated with the situations kids find themselves in on a regular basis. I received a call from a sending school principal informing me that one of my students was in his office. She had been caught making out with another student in the girl's restroom during an all school assembly. Academy kids could attend their parent school activities during the school day if they chose to do so and had their parent's permission. The principal strongly suggested that

I speak with her and her parents regarding the incident and that I make it clear to her that she was no longer welcome on his campus. Knowing E as I did, I decided that the principal's reaction was probably the result of E being totally unrepentant in her responses to both the teacher who discovered her and the Assistant Principal with whom she discussed her transgression. I didn't consider E's situation serious enough to warrant a phone call to my supervisor to let her know what had happened.

However, incidents like E's won't remain secret and will be discussed by the teacher who discovered her with her colleagues in the lounge. It is my experience that when serious incidents involving your kids do occur, a phone call to your supervisor (to give them a heads up) is always a good idea. Always notify your supervisor in situations involving weapons, drugs, assaults, and any time the police come on to your campus for any reason. Your supervisor can't deflect random rumors or gross inaccuracies regarding a situation which occurred if she doesn't have accurate information as to what happened and what your response was. No one likes to be surprised by events in which they have no information and have to formulate an appropriate response to questions or concerns raised by other district officials in response to a frantic phone call from a parent. They can't defend you or your program if they don't have the information necessary to do so. The message here is to communicate frequently with your program's supervisor about what's happening in your building, the good as well as the bad.

The Blue Valley Academy was fortunate to have Dr. S as the program's advocate in the district Office. She was an Assistant Superintendent in the district and headed the district's Educational Services Department which oversaw my program. She believed in the mission of the Alternative program, she believed in our staff, and she believed in me. I went to her for advice when I discovered that one of my students was homeless. M was living in the break room of the McDonald's in which she worked. When the manager found out, he told her she would have to find another place to live. M rented a sleeping space in the laundry room of one of our families for 75.00 a month. She worked two jobs; her mom had her own agenda and was absent. Her dad was incarcerated in a Maryland state prison. I asked Dr. S if she could live in the school until she got back on her feet or until we could contact her mom. She would have a bed, a bathroom, and access to a kitchen. I also requested that she be able to graduate early. She listened as I explained her situation; then, she asked me how old M was. I replied that I thought M would be 16 by the time she graduated. She just put her head on her desk. When she recovered, we talked options. My plan for M to live in the building on a temporary basis was not an option Dr. S was willing to entertain. She didn't panic; we began exploring all the available options. In the end our counselor took M into his home with his family for the reminder of the school year. At the end of the semester M graduated, and shortly afterward, she was married.

For Dr. S. it was about kids, not politics, not ego. She could balance being a human being and enforcing board policy. As a staff we all agreed that if she ever decided to leave the district, it would be time for all of us to fold our tents. We were right. When Dr. S did leave the district, the relationship between myself and the district office changed radically. What had once been a relationship based on doing what's best for kids, now became one in which the Alternative program was viewed as just another district program in need of direction. It was no longer about kid's, it was about process, education by appropriate format. My interactions with the program's new supervisor and the district's new Educational Services Director became an exercise in stamina: (not unlike sitting through teacher education classes). Meetings, reports, more meetings, data production, data analysis, more meetings, paper work. The old days were gone.

All successful Alternative programs need a strong advocate in District Office. If you're lucky you'll have an administrator with whom you can speak your mind (within reason), with whom you can be honest, and one with enough clout to deflect the criticisms of those patrons and colleagues who feel your program is a waste of district resources. The longevity of a program depends on many factors. The aforementioned advocate is of primary importance. Other factors may include:

- **A Perceived Need for Your Program:** For an Alternative program to survive year in and year out it has to strike a chord within the community it serves. It is important that the stakeholders in the district (patrons, students, other administration, and Board members) view the program as having value to the district. Your program must be seen as successful in meeting the needs of the population it was designed to serve and as a necessary component in the districts overall plan to increase its graduation rates while reducing its percentage of dropouts.

- **Having an Innovative, Dedicated, and Resourceful Staff:** An Alternative program must continue to evolve as it experiences staff turnover. Long term staff needs to effectively communicate the mission of the program to incoming staff. In their capacity as instructional leaders, mentors, advisers, and role models, veteran staff must work daily with new staff members to teach them the nuances of the "alternative way" in building relationships and managing the behaviors of at-risk kids. Veteran staff must lead through example in training new staff to understand, embrace, and internalize the philosophies which guide staff interactions with students. In short they must be willing to teach staff new to the program "what to do, how to do it, and when to do it" if they are to become successful Alternative teachers and have a positive impact on the lives of their students.

- **A Secure and Continuous Source of Funding:** In troubled economic times, all teachers understand a district's mandate that "they do more with less." Alternative programs are no exception. However, if your program is constantly fighting for funding on a year to year basis or is perpetually starved for adequate funding, your program will eventually succumb to financial neglect. Staff, students, and parents need to be assured that your program has the verbal as well as the financial support of the Board.

- **A Strong Administrative Presence:** The role of an Alternative principal is many faceted. He/she is the public face of his/her program and as such is responsible for promoting the program, and creating a niche for himself/herself and the program within the district and the community. To accomplish this, Alternative principals must possess the interpersonal skills necessary to effectively communicate their vision and their plan to others and in doing so, motivate others to share in their passion for making a difference in a kid's life.

My most difficult role as a principal was in creating a balance between the expectations of district office while maintaining the independence of my program and that of my staff. Pursuing the "alternative way" in dealing with a restrictive and paradigm driven bureaucracy is challenging at best. As I've stated previously, if you're going to be different, you had better be very good at your job. Superintendents will tolerate variations on a theme from their Alternative principals, but you need to proceed with caution when challenging the conventional wisdom of district administrators. In administrative meetings I assumed the role of gadfly. As an alternative guy, I could get away with offering "alternative approaches" to the status quo thinking of my colleagues. They were by and large company men, espousing the company line in response to issues facing the district. My role was to offer out of the box thinking in response to a problem. It was a comfortable position in which to find one's self. In assuming the personality of the Alternative program, I could project its philosophy; and in doing so, create an understanding among my colleagues, that while I would adhere to the expectations of the district regarding its administrative team, I would meet their expectations in my own way.

If a program is to survive on a long term basis, its principal has to create opportunities for himself to recharge, refocus, and renew his commitment to kids throughout the school year. In the absence of such opportunities, principals find themselves bogged down in the morass of district office meetings, reports, data collection, and the politics of advancement. As a building principal, the days are long. A building principal has significant responsibilities in a variety of areas (medical, civil defense, legal, administrative, therapist to your instructional staff, defender of the faith as prescribed by District Office, surrogate parent to students and parents, and then there is Basketball season. A principals focus is always on the next crisis no matter how big or small; crisis require time and energy. A principal is responsible for everything that goes on in the building, and everything the staff does or doesn't do. As the years wear on, principals tend to smile less due to demands of parents, the job, and the occasional district office official whose approach to everything qualifies him as the poster boy for why teacher unions exist. Thus, the real challenge for an Alternative principal, or any building principal, is to find a means of freeing themselves from the pressures of a district's restrictive bureaucracy. I recommend that every building principal return to the classroom for one period each day, and rediscover the reasons they became an educator in the first place.

As a teaching principal, I always scheduled my class shortly after 10:00 a.m. each day, just when administrative meetings were hitting their stride. Who can argue with a principal needing to leave a meeting, so that he can return to his building and teach his class. A young Assistant Principal once told me that his credibility with kids dropped 90% when he left his classroom and became a full time administrator. Sad but true. Schedule it and you'll do it. Take my advice, teach a class; just one every day. Get reconnected with kids, and your credibility with your instructional staff will improve. You'll not be asking your teachers to do anything that you aren't willing to do yourself. Your perspectives will broaden, and kids will begin to view you in a role unrelated to the office. Free yourself for a short time every day and wear jeans any time you want.

*Note to Alternative Principals: While expounding on the necessities of freeing oneself from the confines of district office politics, I neglected to mention the administrative priorities associated with being an effective, alternative program principal. Like the rules which govern your program, your administrative priorities should be few in number. Keep them simple:

1. Take care of your kids and their families. You may feel that you're dealing with the same people and their issues over and over, but they wouldn't keep calling you if they didn't need you.

2. Support your staff. Listen, encourage, and model the behaviors expected of your staff in your day to day interactions with kids.

3. Meet the expectations of district office. Smile, be cooperative, be on time, and remember to wear your dress jeans on meeting days.

CHAPTER 7

Soap Box Discussions

The following pages contain the author's opinions and reflections on a variety of school related topics. It should be noted that this discussion is more for the author's benefit than yours. However, the author enjoys a good discussion, the ebb and flow of argument, point and counterpoint. Feel free to add your two-cents' worth.

Assessment Score Obsession

A school is only as good as its last test scores. There is no respite from the pressure. Preparation for assessment season is time consuming, narrow in focus (what is not tested is simply not taught), and coercive in nature (perform to AYP standards or else). The pressures of pending assessments are palatable throughout a building. Teachers are anxious, principals nervous about subgroup performance, and kids worried about having to attend remedial summer sessions should they score below a certain level of proficiency. Assessment season begins in February and ends in early May. My youngest daughter announced at dinner one evening that she was so glad assessments were over so that they could do something fun in science again. In response to the demands of Assessment mania, school districts have reduced curricular offerings, mandated common assessments within departments, and worked to ensure that every eleventh grade American History student is exposed to the same content material, presented in the same manner, and at the same pace, as every other eleventh grade American History student throughout the district. We've become France where every kid in the country is taking Algebra at 10:00 a.m. with little variation in content, instructional methods, or text materials. Education by prescription is necessary if a district's primary goal is to ensure that the majority of its kids do well on state assessments, but it's a poor educational practice. The individual needs of kids are no longer priorities for school districts caught in the data driven webs of "testniks" who have hijacked public education. As a result of our nation's high schools are turning out graduates who are proficient in taking tests but who lack substance as persons.

As a principal or teacher your goal is to make every kid's day at school so memorable that they can't wait to share their experiences with someone important to them. However, it is hard for that to happen when assessment schedules dominate classrooms for weeks on end. State assessments are not diagnostic in nature. They do not provide teachers with the information, (in a timely fashion), they need to adjust their curriculums and practices in support of individual student learning styles. Individual assessment scores are returned to a district too late in the semester to make a difference for teachers or students. The reality is that state assessments have evolved as a means of grading respective school districts. School districts are listed by rank in local newspapers and in television broadcasts according to those who made AYP as well as those who did not: the message being that districts making AYP are in some way superior to districts which failed to do so in terms of providing their patrons and students a quality education. District assessment scores have essentially become public relations tools, utilized by realtors to sell homes, and promote the benefits of residing in a community with top notch schools to prospective home buyers. As one superintendent was fond of telling his administrators, people can choose to live anywhere. They choose to live in our district for two reasons: One, we have quality schools as evidenced by our assessment scores; and two, because our district is client- centered. He really meant parent-centered, not necessarily kid-centered.

If a state truly wanted to use assessments as diagnostic tools, they would schedule assessments early in the school year and then again, early in second semester. Providing teachers and counselors with test data in

October would allow them to meet with students and their parents to review the data and construct an Individualized Learning Plan for every student based on their assessment data. Using recent assessment data, teachers could adjust student's ILP to enhance areas of strength, as well as structure in class work to support the areas of the class in which he/she continues to experience difficulty. Everybody wins when assessment data is utilized as the diagnostic tool it was originally intended to be and not as a "club" with which to demoralize and demean the efforts of classroom teachers striving to help their students succeed.

I was attending an administrative meeting in which a district "testnik" was expressing his misgiving about the potential scores of specific district subgroups, and the impact their poor scores would have on the districts overall performance. He was bemoaning the efforts of specific instructors to motivate their students in preparation for the upcoming assessments. A building principal seated across the room from me took issue with the individual's remarks regarding teachers not working hard enough to make sure their kids were ready for assessments. He stated that his special needs son would not make AYP this year; and that in all probability, his son's class would not score high enough to make AYP this year, but he couldn't be prouder of the progress his son had made. He went on to state that his son's teacher had done a wonderful job in motivating his son to believe in himself. The result being that his son had achieved at a level greater than anyone thought possible. He went on to say that his son's teacher would not be recognized for her efforts by her building principal or by the district. She may even be at-risk in terms of her job as the result of her student's poor test performance; but as far as he was concerned, his son had benefited from being in her class. I wanted to get out of my chair and give him a big kiss. What a novel idea — Measuring an individual student's academic growth based on his individual progress throughout his school year. Comparing individual student achievement levels from where they were at the beginning of the school year to their achievement level at the end of the school year. His heartfelt response to the doctrine of AYP at any cost was restating the philosophical premise that the role of public education is to change an individual's life for the better. In short education should be less about the grades an individual earns and more about the kind of person a student becomes as a result of having been exposed to a positive learning environment.

When a district begins to act in the best interest of its kids, rather than politicians, good things begin to happen. The level of trust increases between students, parents, and staff. Students begin to feel comfortable and connected to their school environments, and parents are more willing to invest in a school, and by extension a district, which demonstrates a willingness to embrace all children regardless of individual ability.

Making AYP should not be the sole determining factor in assuming that a district is providing its students with a quality education. Students at one district high school began wearing buttons stating that "I am more than just a test score" on their clothing. A sentiment shared by growing numbers of students, parents, and educators. Common assessments by departments and classroom instruction by prescription results in the creation of learning environments lacking spontaneity, humanity, and individuality, all of which are sacrificed on the altar of collective achievement.

The thought of elected officials dictating through their respective state education offices what constitutes a quality education is ludicrous. Remember these people are politicians. Their status in our society is roughly equivalent to that of a used car salesman; yet, they are entrusted with determining the success (thus value) of respective educational environments in meeting the needs of our students based solely on yearly assessment scores. In reality assessment scores reflect one kid's efforts on a given day, during a specified block of time. Tests do not measure the daily struggles of kids trying to survive the effects of divorce; tests do not measure the progress of newly enrolled immigrant children who don't speak or read the language; and tests do not measure the struggles of kids without a room or a space of their own who must wait until their house clears before they can make their bed on the living room couch for the night, or the issues hunger, abuse, neglect, substance abuse, the list is endless.

Individual student assessment is appropriate and necessary. It should be ongoing throughout a school year and geared to addressing the academic needs of kids. True assessment is one tool in a very large toolbox. Education is all about perspective and determining what's best for kids.

I visited my daughter's school, located on Chicago's west side, one afternoon. Literally hundreds of elementary kids remained in the building to attend after school enrichment and academic support classes. After classes, kids gathered in the school's auditorium for an early evening meal. As I watched kids line up to get their trays, they never stopped interacting with one another or with the staff which served them. It was a time for eating (for some the only meal they would have until they arrived at school the next morning for breakfast) and a time for bonding with caring adults. In watching Em and her colleagues interact with kids, it was clear to me that the role of public education has expanded to become, in a real sense, the last social welfare bastion for kids and their families. Public schools are now responsible for feeding kids, educating them, counseling them, nurturing them, and providing a safe and supervised alternative to dangerous neighborhood streets. Schools provide hope for their future. It's a tough but rewarding mission as evidenced by the smiles of Em's kids as she introduced members of her kindergarten class to my wife and me that afternoon.

In talking with kids about what they remember most about their school experiences, they invariably talk about a teacher, or principal, or a coach who made a lasting, positive impression on them. I have yet to encounter a student, when asked the same question, replied by telling me what he/she scored on a state assessment test.

Wearing Jeans

Public schools are all about appearance, appropriateness of thought, behavior, and dress. The message is one of control. A very smart man once advised me that the true goal of a public school is not education but social control. Somehow, wearing jeans invites feelings among building administrators that staff will be viewed as less effective in their interactions with kids if they are not dressed as "professionals." Staff who wear jeans on a regular basis are suspect when it comes to conveying the preferred message of the school. They may in fact meet for drinks after school, sleep late on Sundays foregoing formal (public) religious affiliations, and refuse to join any professional organizations.

School is serious, it's about image, it's about control, and it's about the one dimensionality our parents suffered from in the 1950's.

For those teachers who conform without question, it's safe, secure, predictable, but lacking in any real educational adventure. Adventure inspires us; it makes us feel alive, and willing to take the next risk. I learned early in my career that if you're going to be different you had better be very good at your job. A word of advice to potential classroom rebels, "never say or do anything in your classroom that is not educationally defensible." If your approach to teaching the district's approved curriculum or your approach to kids is perceived as different from that of your colleagues, you'll have to find a niche within the norms of the traditional school. In my case it was my willingness to take on the district's most difficult students and their parents and get positive results. I was introduced at a party for staff as the teacher "who does a pretty good job handling our criminals."

It's not wise to bite the hand that feeds you (but it's therapeutic to tweak their noses on occasion. Being a "nearly normal" has its rewards. It's not safe or secure, but it builds educational character along with a sense of freedom which proves infectious to your staff and by association your kids.

Teacher Appreciation

It was Teacher Appreciation Week in my district, and the superintendent announced that he would be visiting our building on a specific morning to address my staff. He had to get to every building in the district that day; and as my building was in close proximity to district office, he would visit my staff early on Thursday morning. I met with the staff and notified them of the superintendent's visit on Thursday of this week scheduled for 7:30 a.m. I also told the staff that since the program had no custodian, we would need to get the building ready for his visit. As a staff we were already used to vacuuming our own classrooms and the large group area, emptying our trash cans, and generally taking care of our own spaces. Every staff member with small children, including myself, had to adjust their morning schedules that day. As the staff gathered in our large group area, the superintendent came through our ugly orange doors with a basket of apples, one for each of us, and thanked us for doing our jobs. He then left for another building. His message to my staff was over in a few moments, and he was out the door. Just a little added pressure no one really needs but is part of any job. Moving a child's schedule ahead by thirty minutes on any day can be problematic. This caused everyone to be earlier to breakfast, earlier to dress, and earlier to drop off their children at the sitters. We had some time before the first busses arrived to hang out and chat. None of us felt very appreciated. Our entire morning had been structured around a two-minute appearance. Acknowledging that your staff is doing a good job is a daily thing, but it is especially important during this week. I always told my staff that I wished I could do more than just acknowledge their efforts, that they didn't realize how good they were at what they did. At one time in the district, it was permissible to take your staff out to eat. We could all meet for breakfast or lunch as a small gesture of my appreciation for all that they did. The back to school breakfast was a time for the staff to meet after the summer and catch up before things started speeding up. In-service day lunches and end of the year staff dinners were a perfect way to close out the school year, and show my appreciation for the efforts of the staff throughout the long year. However, the district banned such expenses during a period of budget tightening, and we had to resort to only going out to eat as a staff twice yearly, and only under the guise of a scheduled meeting. It didn't have the same feel as before. If districts are going to celebrate their instructional staff's one week a year, give them something more than platitudes, give them something that makes them believe that you, as an administrator, really do support them and value their contributions.

LEST YOU FORGET I will remind you that your success as an administrator depends largely on the quality of your staff, and their willingness to get the things done you feel are necessary to make things work in your building. Your staff establishes the culture of the school. They spread the gospel on a daily basis, they enforce the routine, and they are in the trenches every day to ensure that their kids are learning and hopefully growing as individuals. Taking the hard work of your staff for granted is a mistake common to many principals but is foolhardy. One district office administrator, speaking to district building administrators, emphasized the importance of getting the movers and shakers on your respective staffs to get (whatever the latest district office initiative was) moving in your buildings. An example of how powerful and necessary an instructional staff is to the overall success of a school's yearly agenda was illustrated very clearly when district office, citing budget restrictions, reduced the number of extended days staff could work and be compensated for by a significant margin. The instructional staffs of the buildings simply stopped volunteering for committee work, or grant writing, or reviewing/writing curriculum in support of core academic areas. The district quickly realized its error in the face of building administrators protests and restored the days to the staff.

Building administrators should consider the following suggestions when thinking of ways in which they can demonstrate their appreciation for the hard work and dedication of their instructional staffs:

- **Schedule In-Service meetings in the mornings, and feed them afterwards.**

   Get accomplished what you need to accomplish, feed them lunch at 11:30, and call it a day. Utilize space in your building to regularly schedule pot luck lunches or breakfasts, and bring baked goods from home on occasion. Your staff needs "comfort food" to get through those days when they wonder (out loud) why they're there.

- **Meet for drinks after school on Friday's and Buy the first round.**

   It's a good way to end the week and provides a relaxed time for staff to sit and talk. Strangely enough most of the conversations tend to be about specific kids, what happened, who was involved, what they did in response, or what needs to be done if it ever happens again? Veteran staffs often find themselves laughing about situations which would bring expressions of horror or tears to those who haven't experienced Alternative students. Over the years alternative staffs have witnessed a lot of good things related to their kids but also a lot of tragedy. Their kids get shot, their babies die, their families fall apart, and they waste their lives in pursuit of a perfect high. As a teacher and a principal you have to continually counsel your staff, and yourself, to seek an emotional balance between the good times and the tragedies which are part and parcel of working with at-risk kids and their families.

- **Utilize your staff as a sounding board for ideas.**
  Your staff should feel comfortable in telling you when they don't agree with you. They serve as your compass in charting the course of your school.

Let them know what you're thinking, ask for their opinions, tell them what's on the horizon from DO and ask for their help in getting it done. Talk everything out at staff meetings. Try to reach a consensus on issues resulting in differing opinions, but ensure that everyone's voice is heard before making a decision which impacts the school as a whole. My staff tended to play at staff meetings. It was often difficult to get them focused and keep them on task. One staff member refused to be part of our normal before and after school gatherings in the office. She was often offended by the conversation, language, and lack of structure as individual staff members sounded off about their day, a student, or parent. Although she wouldn't hang out in the office with the staff, she frequently complained to me that she never knew what was going on in the building. I explained to her that most of that information came forth at the end of day staff gatherings. It was habit for the staff to gather in the office after school to discuss their day. It also served as a quick way for me to dispense information to the staff as a whole rather than go to each person individually with the same information or send impersonal e-mails. She asked me how long she needed to stay each day after school. I explained that she should leave when the conversation was no longer about stuff she considered important to the day to day operations of the program.

The alternative staff was wild and frequently off the wall in many of their comments and conversations with each other. In order to bring some sense of order to our informal and formal meetings, the "three fuck rule" was instituted at all staff meetings. Regardless of what we were discussing or whom we were talking about, staff members collectively could only use the "f" word a total of three times during a meeting. Our Science teacher kept track and would notify us if we had reached our limit or were fast approaching the limit for that day's meeting. In the eleven years we worked together I can only remember one occasion when Mrs. L supported the indiscriminate use of the "F" word at a staff meeting which came as response to my announcing that a creature of district office had been appointed to replace our long term counselor for the upcoming school year. It was obvious by their choice that a new era was dawning for the alternative program; and in response to my announcement, the "three fuck" rule was waived as staff responded from their guts instead of their heads.

- **Pay teachers for all of their unused sick days at the end of each school year.**

  At your districts welcome back convocation, let the entire district know that if they do not need to use their allotted sick leave days during the year, they will be compensated for them in May. Money, even a little money is important to teachers. It's good public relations and sets a positive tone for the year. Many young teachers believe that their sick days are for their optional use, and they should use them regardless if they are ill or not. The promised compensation would reduce the numbers of teachers absent from their classrooms on any given day and provide incentive for them to show up every day.

- **Listen, Encourage, Support, and Advise** your staff whenever you're given the opportunity. Give them what they need to do their jobs and get out of their way. If they need you, they will come and find you.

Substitute Teachers

I always felt that having a sub in my room was more trouble than it was worth. Not that they were bad people, but many had not experienced the ebb and flow of an alternative school environment, and things could get a little out of whack if their personalities and those of the kids did not jell. One substitute told his class that they should be ashamed to attend an alternative school, that they were wasting their time, the district's resources, and that their education was flawed in this environment. Throughout the morning kids kept drifting into my classroom telling me that I needed to go to the CA room and listen to the substitute. I asked them why, and they began to tell me what he had said about their school and about themselves. They were upset and wanted me to do something about it. I spoke to as many kids as I could find in the hallways regarding the negative comments the substitute was making in class towards both the program and its students and basically got the same story from a variety of kids. I went into the CA classroom prior to the beginning of the next class and asked the substitute how things were going? I told him that I had had several student complaints regarding his comments about the Academy program and asked him what he had said to students. He began to tell me that he was just stating his opinion regarding the program and the students who attended here. I asked him if the lesson plans left by the teacher included his assessment and opinion of the program and its students? I explained to him that he was here to implement the instructor's lesson plans not to demean the program or its students. I asked him if he could refrain from giving his personal opinions for the remainder of the day and follow the instructor's lesson plans. If that were not possible he needed to tell me now and leave. He asked me if he should leave, and I replied only if he felt himself incapable of following the lesson plans and refraining from any further commentary. He was quiet for a moment and then said he would remain for the rest of the day. On the flip side we were blessed with three great subs which could be relied on to enter a classroom and take care of business without any major issues day in and day out. They liked our kids and were comfortable in their own skins which made for a fairly laidback environment in which kids could function successfully. They made my life a lot easier, and I appreciated their willingness to come whenever we needed them.

Medication Nation

"I forgot to take my meds today" was a common refrain from students sitting in my office as the result of their having been sent out of class. We would have discussions about medication maintenance and the possibility of bringing a supply to leave with our nurse in case they forgot again. Phone calls to their parents would often center around their child's individual issues and of their attempts to modify their students challenging behaviors, both at home and in school, with a combination of prescription drugs and therapy. Frequently, parents would state that they were having trouble getting their son or daughter to take their medications, as they often stated that they didn't like how it made them feel. Adjusting individual medications or beginning a new medication series would result in many kids either being off the walls in terms of their ability to focus or unable to keep their heads off of their desks and their eyes open during class. During enrollment interviews, parents would inform me that their child had been diagnosed with ADHD and was currently taking medication for their condition. They wanted me to know about their kid's condition and for me to alert the instructional staff to be aware of their child's disability. I would listen politely and then state that nearly every student in our program was diagnosed as having ADHD in some form or another, and that our staff was experienced in providing all students with classroom environments in which they could succeed regardless of their disabilities.

There are many schools of thought regarding the increasing numbers of brain altering medications prescribed for teenagers who are experiencing difficulties in their public school environments. As a classroom teacher and principal it has been my experience that those kids I most often saw in my office for issues resulting from their being out of emotional control (and thus out of instructional control) needed their medication on a daily basis. It was painfully obvious to everyone that their behavioral responses to provocations imagined or otherwise were more positive on the days when they took their medications then on days when they didn't. Some educators consider the huge increases in medicated teens as a matter of simple convenience on the part of parents, whose own issues have yet to be resolved and who have few emotional and mental resources to give their children, when they begin to encounter similar difficulties. Stories, in my district, of affluent parents downing out their toddlers for the afternoon so that they could pursue their social interests uninterrupted and undisturbed for a few hours were rampant. I would rather believe that the increase in the number of prescriptions written for public school kids is a direct result of parents, family doctors, and counselors having an increased knowledge and understanding of how adolescent brains function; thus increasing the understanding of specific adolescent behaviors, causation, and treatment — expanding knowledge and awareness results in a wider variety of treatment options available to parents and therapists. Parents who have weathered the storm of their adolescent's shifting moods, unpredictable behaviors, and resulting school issues are looking for answers and hopefully solutions, to the issues which dominate their children's lives and impact their families on a daily basis.

On more than one occasion distraught parents have sat in my office baring their souls over their inability to build a connection between themselves, their family, and their son or daughter. Many have finally reached a point where they feel that their focus solely on the problems surrounding one of their children is having an adverse impact on their other children and the family as a whole. They are tired and worn down by the constant issues surrounding the one child and feel that they now need to act to save their other children. One parent stated that her son was currently incarcerated but that she had refused the court's decision to return him to her custody, as she just needed some peace, and knew for once, where he was.

In theory, prescribing medications which chemically alter an adolescent's brain activity is a short-term response to dealing with the greater issues associated with strong displays of emotion, depression, anxiety, inability to focus, or anger issues. In conjunction with ongoing therapy and strong parental involvement, the potential that all will benefit and find a measure of peace is positive. Eventually, all teens mature; and the hope is that whatever issues are now dominating their child's current life, will diminish as their child matures into young adulthood.

Alternative educational environments play an important role in helping troubled students find ways to achieve personal, social, and academic success and hopefully reduce their reliance on prescription medications over the long run. The positive relationships built between a student and teacher, a non-judgmental and accepting school environment, and the willingness of capable, student- centered adults to interact with kids outside of a classroom can do much to counter the effects of student misbehavior, subsequent academic issues, and the reliance on chemical solutions in response to ongoing, individual problems. Positive based behavioral interventions by caring teachers provide kids with opportunities to practice behaviors and approaches to problem solving which go beyond their familiar patterns of dealing with a situation or in assuming behavioral roles which lessen their emotional or personal stake in finding a workable solution to their problems. A willingness for kids to take the risks necessary to change those things about themselves which reinforce barriers to their success is a major first step for many. This is a direct outgrowth of their trust, their realization that they need to make changes, and of their faith in the caring adults who acknowledge their situations while providing behavioral options, encouragement, and the structure kids need to truly change their perceptions of themselves.

Homework

My last alternative program served the populations of four senior high schools in a self- described "college prep district." The district was affluent and proud of its record of graduates who went on to post secondary education. Homework was seen by many in the district as a necessary precondition to an individual student's success in college. All teachers were expected to give homework and the vast majority of them did, every night. Imagine coming home from your job knowing that you still had two hours of additional work to accomplish before starting the process all over tomorrow. A significant majority of students referred to the program were not well organized, not good note takers, not auditory learners, not good readers, and not inclined to do their homework. Those that did do their homework seemed unable to get it turned in; and if they managed to turn it in, it was always late, and thus no credit was given in the class. Any student who got behind on a week's worth of homework assignments found themselves in a very deep and dark hole. Homework assignments in the majority of core curriculum classes constituted fifty-per cent of an individual student's grade in the course. It mattered not that a student had passed every exam or that they were frequent contributors in class discussions. If they didn't do their homework, they would not pass the class. Parents came to my office looking for help with their child who, although bright, was failing his or her classes because they refused to do the assigned homework. They had spoken to their child's teachers, counselors, and administrators to no avail. The educational value of homework was unassailable. They complained to me that they had given up fighting with their child every night about whether the homework was completed. They had heard that the alternative program did not assign homework. I told them that was true as we expected everything assigned by the instructor to be completed and turned in prior to the student leaving campus at the end of the day. If, for any reason, the student had not completed the assigned work in class that day, then the assignment was considered homework to be turned in the next school day. A large number of our students, who were referred to the program by their parent schools for chronic academic failure, were in fact very intelligent students who just refused, for whatever reason, to play the homework game.

"If I can pass the exams why should I do the homework?" It seemed like a fair question to me when asked by a bright eyed, eleventh-grade girl whose parents were in my office to discuss the possibility of her enrollment in our program. She had already told her parents that if she wasn't accepted into the program, she would just drop out. She was failing the majority of her classes that semester and didn't see the point of continuing at her parent school. Her parents had told her that she was capable of passing her classes, and whether she did her homework or didn't do it, was her responsibility. They were tired of the fight. The result being that she didn't change anything about her approach to her classes and was now entering her third year of high school as a seventeen-year-old, first semester sophomore in terms of academic credits earned. She attended school most days just to hang out with her friends, not to make the effort necessary to resolve her academic issues. She was at a tipping point in her high school career, and her parents were desperate never believing that their daughter would be in danger of not graduating from high school. The conversation focused on what she would do differently should she be accepted into the program. I explained to her that the expectation here was that she would do all assigned work not just the assignments she chose to complete. She could make up lost ground as the result of our block schedule in which she could earn eight credits for the year and pick up extra academic credits if she enrolled in elective classes at her parent school each semester. The big question she needed to answer was if she visualized herself walking across the stage one day with a diploma in her hand? If the answer to that question was" yes," the alternative school would provide her a pathway towards meeting her goal. However, if she was just here to placate her parents and had no real intention of doing anything differently, she would not be here long and would have wasted both her time and mine.

The bottom line was that she could conceivably graduate with her original class if she kept her word, made an honest effort in class every day, and followed the plan. Her parents remained quiet as I asked her point blank what she intended to do. They were relieved when she stated that she would like to graduate with her class and that she was willing to do the things necessary for that to happen. She had given me her word, and I explained to both her and her parents that she could expect me to keep my word when given and that I expected no less from her. As I walked them to my office door, I reminded the young lady that the past was the past and nobody here cared what she had done or hadn't done in her parent school. However, when she walked through those ugly orange doors on the first day of school, she was expected to take care of business and do her job. We all shook hands as she and her parents thanked me for my time. As I walked back to my office I thought, "another homework refugee in from the cold."

Board Meetings

Over my career I've attended hundreds of them. They usually ran late, were mostly civil, and for the most part board members focused on doing the business necessary to run the district. As a district patron or employee attending the meetings, you never get to hear the good stuff which always happened in private, behind closed doors, in Executive Session. You can read the Board minutes the next day and find out what their decision was regarding a specific issue, but you're never there for the give and take. Only when an individual's job is in the balance or a popular program is being cut and the public is emotionally involved in the outcome, do things tend to get interesting at Board meetings. When a large crowd is anticipated and the numbers of patrons signed up to make public comments is lengthy, the potential for drama lasting long into the night is a real possibility. Some Boards of Education truly have balls. A large suburban district's Board of Education and District Office Administration took on a very vocal group of parents who attempted to highjack the districts Communication Arts Curriculum and control its reading content for high school students. They were not content in talking with their sons or daughters teachers to request that their children be given an alternative book to read for the class, they sought to control the content of reading matter for every parent's child. They were vocal and organized. They sought to rid the district's secondary schools of books containing inappropriate passages, sexual innuendo, offensive language, and themes deemed inappropriate for teens. Our Board took them on and won. What the parents advocating censorship didn't seem to grasp was that individual parents and their kids were capable of deciding those issues for themselves; and resented others, no matter how well intentioned, attempting to make those decisions for them. Individual parents may disagree with an assigned reading book, but are capable of communicating their own concerns and making the decisions which they feel is best for their own kids regarding assigned reading material. "Make those decisions for your kid, don't make them for mine" seemed to be the crux of the argument directed against the parents demanding that the list of current books recommended by the CA department be screened for inappropriate content. If a book was found to contain such material it should be removed not only from the districts approved reading list but also from every district library shelf as well. The group expended a lot of energy and emotion in making their case in the media, but common sense prevailed; and people rejected the premise that exposure to many different perspectives is dangerous to the growth and development of young minds.

What students, their parents, school personnel, and patrons think is of little interest to some sitting Boards of Education. They are more interested in what their administrators are thinking, talking about, and doing. They see their role as second guessing their administrative staffs on issues regarding discipline, teacher effectiveness, conduct, assignment of academic standing, grades, and the application of building policies in response to specific situations. District patrons dissatisfied or in disagreement with the answers they receive from building principals over specific issues are able to access the back channel directly to Board members as a means of pressing their case. Mr. B was one such Board member. He was not a snappy dresser, didn't come off as overly intelligent, and was not particularly good looking; yet somehow he became Board President and along with his posse systematically undermined and destroyed a very talented, effective, and forward thinking district administrative team. Micromanagement of the district by Mr. B and his supporters eventually lead to the dismissal of the superintendent and the Board voting not to void or buy out his contract. Essentially, they refused him the opportunity to seek other employment while he remained under contract to the district. He spent the next school year in limbo waiting for the opportunity to once again lead a district,— Bad day at Black Rock stuff.

In another district our administrative team spent many an emotional moment formulating the district's response to two female students who openly declared their love and affection for one another. The issue seemed to hinge on both student and parent complaints regarding the outed girls being in the same locker room as "straight" girls, their holding hands in the hallways, and other public displays of affection observed by both faculty and students during the school day. One possible response discussed was to suspend the two girls and mandate that they receive counseling as a condition of their re-admission to school. Cooler heads prevailed, and it was determined that the students and their parents should be reminded of the district's policy on public displays of affection between students while on school property or during the school sponsored/supervised activities. Both the girls and their parents would be asked to meet with the school's counselor and building administrator to discuss the policy and what the school's position would be should the girls violate the Board's policy on this matter in the future. Other meetings focused on the outcome of the student body election for Homecoming King and Queen. The winning queen candidate was very pregnant; and the Superintendent felt that perhaps having a pregnant queen, presented to the public during the half time festivities, might send the wrong message to the voting public. He simply suggested that the votes be recounted with the results being adjusted in favor of the runner up candidate. Another evening was spent in a spirited discussion of whether the district should honor the transcript request of a former student who had left the district to pursue his GED. A Board member proposed that the student in question re-enroll in the district for a semester to put in the seat time required of all students prior to his receiving his transcript from the district. Comments were made concerning the legality of the GED as an indication of an individual's having completed the academic requirements necessary to enroll in a Junior College. After a period of intense discussion, the student's request for his transcript was granted. Between the Board's discussion of milk prices or in viewing and discussing the new football uniforms, the business of the district concluded at approximately midnight. They took a dinner break at 10 p.m. with a meal provided by ladies from the community. The meals were great. Real food on real plates. After the meetings were adjourned for the evening, Board members stood around outside the front entrance of the high school and talked. Sometimes they would pile into their vehicles and drive the forty-five minutes (one way) to a truck stop in Peculiar, MO to have breakfast. I drove home most nights after the meetings, arriving at my home after 1a.m. in the morning and then getting up at 6 a.m. for the return drive to work. It's a good thing board meetings were scheduled only once a month.

Meeting Season

A schedule of all administrative meetings that building administrators were expected to attend at district office came in your "back to school packet" along with the goals of the district for the year (survival was not considered a valid goal for either teacher or administrator). District Office expected energy, enthusiasm, and commitment to the district's plan from its administrators. A district office "who-ha" came by the table where I was sitting during an administrative meeting asked me if "I was pumped"? I responded "about what"? She just looked at me and left for more fertile hobnobbing ground. I just wanted to get through the next three hours and get back to my building. I never felt comfortable at administrative functions. It was my own fault. I just couldn't relax around the majority of school administrators. As an alternative classroom teacher, I was conditioned to view the majority of school administrators as more trouble than they were worth. I viewed them in the context of the "uncle daddy syndrome". Administrators were individuals who came into your classroom twice a year to observe and gather material which would later become part of your yearly evaluation. I never saw them at any other time during the year unless they had gotten a phone call from someone in the community or district, involving one of my kids, and they felt it necessary to come over and talk with the staff about the situation, and the expected fallout. When I became an administrator, it was always in conjunction with my starting an Alternative program in a respective district. In some districts I was considered an Assistant Principal, in others a building Principal whose program was placed on an equal footing with the other high schools in the district. I know it sounds negative, but I never wanted to be a part of a district as a whole, parity with the sending schools was simply a myth. We lived in different worlds; and in all honesty, I never wanted to be part of their world. One district office official with whom I was engaged in a discussion asked me which "district I worked for?" I replied that I worked for the same one he did, but there were other options in dealing with a situation other than simply adhering to the approved district line. My loyalty was first to my staff rather than the district which employed me. Perhaps that was the reason for the "disconnect". We viewed our roles as administrators differently. They were company men and district centered. I was a kid's first guy and program centered.

One building administrator stated in casual conversation that she had spent weekends and many days at school working on her building's School Improvement Plan. It was thirty-five pages in length and had consumed a large amount of her time to write. My Alternative program was also required to write a School Improvement Plan, even though we were considered a program and not a school. It was that parity thing again. The district insisted that all buildings follow an approved format for submitting their final plans to Dr. M. I submitted our plan to his office and was thankful to be done with it. Dr. M took the Alternative programs submission to my supervisor stating that it did not meet the criteria he had set forth for all buildings nor was my programs plan presented in the appropriate format. Dr. S reviewed our plan and said that "it looked exactly like a plan that would serve an alternative program." She sent the idiot boy packing, and my staff and I sang her praises and toasted her at our next choir practice. It was just a process like turning in a term paper for a class. Once completed, I put a copy in my office desk and never looked at it again unless pressed by district office. I could never stop thinking like a classroom teacher and become a true believer. As a staff we discussed, updated, and implemented our School Improvement Plan on a daily basis, during our informal meetings, before and after school. I did my best to hide my true feelings regarding administrative meetings but failed to do so on occasion. A former board member referred to me as being "arrogant, smug, and disinterested." She was right. I put her words on t-shirts and gave them to my staff. We all laughed, but her words accurately identified the mind set of many Alternative teachers and principals when dealing with district office agendas. I am a teacher first and a district administrator second. I was a district administrator for twenty-five years, but never left my classroom or quit thinking like a teacher.

I scheduled my class at 10:15 a.m. so that I had a valid excuse to leave meetings, however, one morning Dr. M followed me out of a meeting and into the hallway stating that a lot of important things were discussed in the last thirty to forty minutes of these meetings. My response was that kids came first, and I was responsible for twenty at-risk kids in the next fifteen minutes and needed to be in my classroom ready to teach. His meeting had started at 7:00 a.m. that morning, it was now 9:55 a.m., and he still had thirty to forty minutes more to go. On another occasion he told me that he had forgotten to notify me of a meeting; although, he stated that I probably didn't care. He was right, I didn't. He and I never saw eye to eye on anything, and I tweaked his nose every chance I got. Throughout my tenure in the district I never met an individual so consumed with advancing his own career. I never truly felt comfortable as an administrator. They always dressed as if they were going to church while I had to prompt myself to remember to wear underwear on big meeting days.

Kids First

As a motto it's short and sweet. As an educational philosophy it's all encompassing. It's the gold standard by which every interaction, every conversation, and every action is measured at the end of every school day. As educators we have one true mission; to make a positive difference in a kids life every day. Embracing the philosophy requires every educator to care more than anyone else whether all students are personally, socially, and academically successful. For those educators whose priorities are less about kids and more about the politics of personal advancement, do the profession a great service. Go sell insurance.